The Healing of Teddy Bears

Creating an Imaginative Faith

Best wishes,

Don Nickerson

DON L. NICKERSON

The Healing of Teddy Bears: Creating an Imaginative Faith

Published by Wheatmark™

610 East Delano Street, Suite 104, Tucson, Arizona 85705 U.S.A.

www.wheatmark.com

Publisher's Cataloging-In-Publication Data
(Prepared by The Donohue Group, Inc.)

Nickerson, Don L.
  The healing of teddy bears : how to create an imaginative faith / by Don L. Nickerson.

  p. ; cm.

  ISBN-13: 978-1-58736-785-4 (hardcover)
  ISBN-13: 978-1-58736-784-7 (pbk.)
1. Faith. 2. Metaphysics. 3. Spiritual life. I. Title.

BL626.3 .N53 2007

204.4   2007920768

CONTENTS

For Linda, life companion on the journey

An Introduction to

The Healing of Teddy Bears

Creating an Imaginative Faith

by Don L. Nickerson

At the time of its first printing in May of 2007, one Massachusetts reviewer, The Reverend Michael Robinson, understood how radical *The Healing of Teddy Bears* was. He said, in a September review in *The New Bedford Standard Times*, "Hang onto your seat belts!" Poet and physicist James Cox also hinted at the book's radical character when he declared *Teddy Bears* to be an "unexpected, wild ride." And retired businessman Clifford Winter said the book "would be bound to create controversy."

It was exactly that kind of reader understanding I had hoped for, one that would invite dialogue and create an excited openness to the possible meanings of "faith." *Teddy Bears* is not a finished product with vacuum-packed ideas, but one possessing a curious kind of organic character, wherein its concepts are capable of <u>being</u> transformed, as well as transforming. It is a document I have discovered competent to exert further changes of consciousness in myself, for example, as I re-read it.

Readers must not be misled by the conversational tone of this book, or by the author's intentional "failure" to support the concepts he puts forth by appeals to various authorities and extensive footnotes. The conversational tone is intended to be engaging, and to avoid intentional inflammation or polarization. While the book's ideas *are* often unusual, and may appear radical to our mind-sets, the book itself has a heart-intention, of being open, exploratory, accepting, even embracing. I hope it is possible for most readers to "get" this paradoxical intention, the desire of the author to engage the reader rather than alienate, and at the same time invite the reader to breathe deeply into concepts that may appear sometimes strange, or possibly even offensive at first reading.

What of the failure to cite authorities, and to footnote? Also intentional. I intend to <u>underline</u> what is likely the *most radical* concept of this book, my encouragement to the reader to move *inward*, to their own hearts, intuition and creative imagination to find the ground for their personal beliefs and lives.

At the age of 19, my very first reliance on inward experimentation formed the beginnings of my spiritual beliefs. My inward experiments had nothing to do at that point with any established religion or external authority. Nor did they have anything to do with my background, growing up in a home where religion was never discussed, and effectively ignored. While I never forgot my 19-year-old "beginnings" based on inward experience, for the following 15 years or so I entered a seminary world of reliance on externalized authority—biblical "infallibility"—followed by biblical-Christology authority.

My return to a faith of internal experience was eventually nurtured by energy-consciousness, heart-consciousness, and increasing trust in the immediacy of body-mind intuition. Which is not to say there were not conflicts between the two systems of external and internal during the final years of my 15-year sojourn with externalized authority. There were conflicts, and they raised red flags. However, I was able to compartmentalize effectively enough to persist within the system until the breakup of my marriage and family propelled me into extensive psychotherapy. From that point forward it was only a matter of time until I would become conscious of the God within, and of my identification with Being.

Reliance on internal consciousness as a ground for personal authority brings with it a certain liberation. For one thing, it leads to a much larger appreciation of all human beings and of what is often the uniqueness of their belief systems, including atheism and agnosticism—which *are* belief systems. For another, we are delivered from any necessity to "prove" our beliefs are "the right ones." While not denying the persuasiveness of our experience, nor its potency, experiential beliefs are not "fixed." They are fluid and dynamic, and most of us hope our egos are not overly attached to what must, by its nature, be subject to possible change. Some of us are excited by the dynamic character, the moving energy of inner consciousness, but such awareness is bound to be very threatening for those who *are* attached to systems of beliefs that provide exactness, unvarying continuity and security.

Teddy Bears, then, is not about proving anything or quarreling. But it does raise questions, it is a statement about a certain kind of spiritual positioning of consciousness, and it is an invitation to *explore* an inward, non-rational way of seeing things.

Let me speak again about this book's first chapter. It is important to state that it records an experience of the author's practice of his faith. It isn't a testimony of anything else, unless it would be an invitation to the reader to do more "exploring" of the power of his or her own inwardness of heart. In a small Tucson critique group I was in at the time I wrote *Teddy Bears*, one of its lovely members said, "Prove it!" when

I read the account of Teddy's healing. Well, to enter that territory, of "proving," is to stand on a different ground of authority than inward experience. It is to commit exclusively to science and reason. I believe it is a huge mistake for persons of faith to *leave* the ground of the heart in what I think of as the futile attempt to prove anything at all related to faith. In my estimation, for example, it seems useless as well as foolish to try to "prove" that God exists, let alone prove any of the other aspects of inner consciousness that have become important in our spiritual journey. Let's leave to the scientists what they do best, and be ready to learn from their discoveries…and sometimes even from their theories. But in the meantime, let us persist as well in the adventures of inward faith… the heart and imaginative creativity.

It is true that scientific theory at times seems to pose the possibility of supporting, or confirming, certain beliefs originally discovered through processes of deep inwardness, such as Mongolian shamanism, Taoist movement energy consciousness, or Buddhist meditation. For more than 30 years, for example, scientists have been able to photograph energy fields that surround the human body and plants. Yet, a fear of what is not obvious persists. There are still intelligent people who call energy consciousness "hocus-pocus." So, oddly, we have entire eastern cultures accustomed for centuries to the practice of inner consciousness, and a western culture still dominated by slavish reliance on science and reason. And, I might add, dominated by fear of loss of rational control.

The most radical concept of the book is, indeed, in the very first chapter, where I convey my personal belief that heart faith on my Teddy Bear's behalf resulted in his molecular transformation. I don't make "claim" that happened. Wouldn't I be making a claim to authority if I did? Wouldn't I be falling into the deadly trap of trying to make my particular faith experience normative for others? Would not my own ego be attached to a need to "prove" it *really* happened? In fact, I have no desire to have the chapter read as an attempt to prove anything, or to persuade readers a similar result might be re-produced by others, or even under other circumstances by me. The story stands on its own as a report of a certain experiment of faith, a certain engagement of heart, and a belief that a "healing" occurred. I tell the story to encourage readers to go beyond the boundaries of how their minds ordinarily think about things, and see what happens when both heart and imagination are engaged with life. It is important to approach such experiments without expectations, and to keep the ego out of it as much as possible. The ego *always* needs to prove things, to be right, to be center stage. It is the heart that is competent to love, and to stay open to possibilities, and to what "is."

Thirty years ago, when I had become most deeply committed to inward consciousness and openness, I was fortunate enough to study with a brilliant spiritual teacher, Brugh Joy, during a two-week retreat. One phase of the retreat involved a 24-hour fast and an individual, silent climb into surrounding hills through and over large rocks. Brugh suggested that as we climbed we become aware the rocks could respond to us energetically, actually supporting various parts of our bodies out of their own consciousness, if we were aware of that possibility and yielded to it. I found it to be exactly the case. I had to exert less energy when I stopped thinking of the rocks as "obstacles,' and began to think of those I clambered over as assisting me in my climb.

I had probably not thought of that rock-climbing incident consciously since, until I read an article in the November 18th, 2007 *New York Times* magazine section. Written by Jim Holt, he called his article, "Mind of a Rock." Unlike my book, Mr. Holt freely quoted scientists who theorized about the pervasive nature of consciousness. In conclusion he wrote,

"At a microlevel (a rock) consists of an unimaginable number of atoms connected by springy chemical bonds, all jiggling around at a rate that even our fastest super-computer might envy…You might draw the moral that the universe is, and always has been, saturated with mind, even though we snobbish Darwinian-replicating latecomers are too blinkered to notice."

There are several other radical concepts in *Teddy Bears*, but none so radical as its commitment to inwardness of heart, imagination, and intuitive consciousness. Once we move in that direction we have to be prepared to let go of all of the attachments our hearts require of us.

There are a number of persons I would like to thank for their contributions to the writing and/or second printing of *Teddy Bears*. Two eagle-eyed readers, a neighbor-friend Steven Kudla, and my sister-in-law, Dell Ann Dyar, humbled us by finding errors we have corrected with this printing. My long-time friend from bible college days, Clifford Winter of Lexington, Kentucky, found me, and my manuscript, after an almost 50-year lapse. It was he who urged me to put the essays into print, and who made possible its printing. His enthusiasm and support are incalculable.

My wife, Linda Larsen, read every chapter through many revisions, engaged their concepts, and made vital corrections to the final copy. She is a very "significant other"! My thanks, too, to others who read portions of the manuscript: Cliff Winter, his daughter Lynn of Louisville, Kentucky, and Tom Cannan, Ed Donovan and Dick and Ruth Ann Hamilton from the SaddleBrooke community in Tucson, Arizona.

The Writer's Workshop of SaddleBrooke has been a place of great support, friendship and inspiration for many years. They, along with the

St. Philip's Writers of Tucson, were patient and helpful in their listening, and unwavering in their confidence in my thought and writing.

The touching and faithful cover art that portrays my childhood "Teddy" and the lovable teal dragon, Shemoosing, is the work of an exceptional SaddleBrooke artist, Kay Sullivan. I'm so pleased her work could grace the cover of *Teddy Bears*.

There were a number of early readers of the first printing who gave me permission to quote their comments about the book. As this goes to press, I hope to include a few of those comments, and thank all who commented. Their observations, if not here, are at the web site for the book, www.thehealingofteddybears.com.

Finally, I have appreciated the close counsel, effort and support of my publisher, Wheatmark of Tucson, represented especially through Grael Norton. Lori Sellstrom, book editor, was a great help in assisting me to put together the kind of book of which I could be proud.

I am encouraging dialogue with readers. Please feel free to email: lindontucson@aol.com.

CHAPTER 1

On the Healing of Teddy Bears

When I was in my 50's, my mother gave me a few small items she had kept from my infancy and childhood. She had somehow saved them through her two marriages and several house moves. One was a pair of leather baby shoes. Another was a teddy bear. I put them away in a box until one day my youngest daughter discovered them and asked if she could have the teddy bear for a while. I agreed, but said I would want it back when I moved to another home.

After my wife, Linda, and I moved to a Portland, Oregon, condominium, I thought of the teddy bear. I retrieved it from my daughter and put it on top of a cabinet in the corner of our bedroom, nestled with two of Linda's stuffed animals and one of mine, a little teal-hued dragon. I was quite taken by what an interesting and disparate collection they made.

My wife had given me the teal dragon, which I decided was a "she," when I was briefly hospitalized for a pacemaker replacement. It had white fuzz where her "third eye" might have been. She also had pink wings and ears. Her eyes appeared—well—cheerful, happy. She was a colorful, whimsical dragon. I named her Shemoosing. A quite strange name, I thought, until I observed that "She" referred to the feminine, and "moosing" likely to a moose, which had been my totem animal for over 30 years.

I don't know when I began to notice Teddy, as I had named him. Perhaps it was when I playfully struck up lively conversations with Shemoosing, and belatedly realized I had never paid the slightest attention to Teddy. He was just "there." He had no function. A lot of his fuzz had worn off, and he was just one shade short of appearing to be a bare skin stretched over his stuffing. Because he didn't look or feel soft, he wasn't cuddly. One of his legs looked as if it were just dangling from where it was joined to his hip, basically disconnected. So there he sat, requiring that I prop him up solidly against the wall so he wouldn't collapse. Shemoosing, on the other hand, standing on all four of her legs and feet was very steady, her pretty green fur fluffy and layered. Of course, Teddy was over 60 years old. Shemoosing, a playful child-dragon, was only two or three.

A process began in my consciousness when I *noticed* I had been attending Shemoosing and ignoring Teddy. The next thing I observed in my consciousness was that I was beginning to see, or believe, Teddy had "been through a lot." What he and I would eventually experience began with this seed of sympathy for his fate. Surely I had been aware of his eyes all along! But maybe not. Maybe I didn't want to see the detachment that lurked in his glass eyes. Yes, that was it. Teddy was disengaged from me, and energetically separated from his stuffed animal companions. He was no longer in this world, except for his frayed and injured body.

When I looked more closely into Teddy's eyes, I could see a hint of something else: sadness. He was very, very sad. Hurt perhaps. My heart opened up more. How could I have ignored him all this time? When Mother gave Teddy to me in my late 50's, I confess I didn't really "see" him, in the sense of a spark of recognition or feeling. Mother had to tell me that this stuffed bear was the teddy bear of my infancy and early childhood. I had no sense or vision of ever having held him; yet, I must have. Mother would have seen to it. There was no way she was going to spend money for a perfectly good teddy bear and have me reject it. She would have put it in my arms and insisted. So, I must have held Teddy.

It's entirely possible the truth between Teddy and me was not that way at all. The forgotten truth may have been that in my private, secret world, I clung to Teddy, talked to him well into the night. I might have been affectionately bonded with him once upon a time. But if so, all that was wiped out, all memory of such connectedness between him and me had been erased. Up to this point, ever since Mother returned Teddy, I had been as disconnected from Teddy as he had been from me and the world around him. I was very affected in realizing our mutual estrangement. I felt my failure to notice even the slightest thing about Teddy had to be strange, possibly pathological, especially in light of my recent child-like enjoyment of a colorful stuffed dragon like Shemoosing. Did Teddy notice how easily I smiled, sometimes laughed or grinned, during my brief encounters with Shemoosing? If he noticed, did it intensify his own feelings of neglect and abandonment?

I want to thank my readers for staying with me for such a fantasy-filled story, when I attribute human qualities to stuffed animals, and report encounters and conversations with them. But there is a point to my story. First, everything I have recorded really did happen. It is my history, my perception of the nature of reality. I really *did* talk to my stuffed animals. For a period of time I "saw," or projected onto them, if you prefer, elements of a vivid imagination. If my behavior *was* projective, I attributed to them aspects of myself, split off into the "happy" dragon and the "sad" teddy bear.

I would be quite foolish, with my training and background as a psychotherapist and teacher of Gestalt Process, to deny the possibility of projective explanations. After all, I obviously and intentionally humanized my stuffed animals. At the very least I have given them emotional capabilities that one assumes childhood stuffed animals simply cannot possess. But let me move on.

Once I came to believe, imaginatively or otherwise, that Teddy was both detached and sad, a conclusion I reached by looking into his eyes, I decided I no longer wanted to be party to his detachment. I would not ignore him. In fact, I was determined to engage Teddy. I began to talk to him, telling him I was sorry I had neglected him for such a long time. I told him I loved him, and asked if I could hold and cuddle him. While I didn't actually *hear* Teddy him give me permission, there was some way in which I felt an energy of his consent.

I picked him up and held him close to my heart. Then I kissed his rough little cheek, nuzzled him, put his snout into the cradle made by my shoulder and my neck. I stayed that way for a time, breathing in, breathing out, sending heart energy of love, my arms staying soft but supportive. We maintained close contact for some time, until I gently lifted Teddy away from me so I could support his body in both hands and look into his face and eyes. His damaged leg dangled down to the side of my left hand, and I carefully lifted it up so it also was supported within my hands. I looked into his eyes, and he was looking back. He looked puzzled, as if he were trying to figure something out. The sadness was gone. He was no longer detached, but obviously he needed time to absorb what was happening between us. I drew him to my breast briefly, then held him out from me so I could talk to him, face to face. I told him I was going to put him down so he could rest, and that he would be all right because he was going to be with Shemoosing and the animal friends belonging to Linda. He seemed to understand. I told him I was going to be fixing dinner, but I would be back. I was not going to leave him forever. Then I placed him right in the midst of all his friends and left.

That was not the end of the story, of course. I did come back later. I picked him up, and could not help but notice right off that he was making energetic contact with me. He was engaging, not detaching. While there was not a lot of life as yet in his eyes, much of the expression of puzzlement had faded, and all of his sadness. He was really, really present. Over the next few days, as I would look at him when going to bed, or rising in the morning, he would be looking at me, no longer staring off into space. His eyes would follow me. I tried to position him among the other stuffed animals so he would be braced and able to see better what was going on around him.

For some time after the experiences I have described, I would intentionally make contact of various kinds with Teddy, especially eye contact. His eyes increasingly carried more energy, in my opinion. One could not say his eyes were filling with affection, and certainly they were not filling with humor, but they were lively, rather than detached. He belonged and knew it. He belonged with me, he belonged in the house, and he belonged with the stuffed animals who had become his supportive companions.

I have not reported to you thus far, how my wife, a clinical psychologist, was a party to the events I have described. I brought her into my experience with Teddy early on, after I had realized how detached he was, and before I tumbled to the reality I had been ignoring him ever since Mother returned him to me. Without giving any verbal cues to

Linda as to how I was seeing Teddy, I would ask her what she saw. We concurred in what we saw in Teddy's eyes. With each transition in what I believed to be Teddy's changing energetic state, I would call Linda into the room to tell me what she saw. She could see the transitional affective states in Teddy's eyes, too. The easiest explanation for all this, of course, is that I first hypnotized myself into believing these changes of affective and boundary states were occurring in Teddy, and then Linda fell under the spell of my consciousness, and saw Teddy as I did. There is absolutely no way to deny this might well have been the case. But it is not what I believe, and this takes us to the point, or points, of the lengthy story I have told.

A clinical psychologist friend of mine is specializing in writing about how the cells and circuits of the brain can actually be changed through certain attitudes and techniques. When I told her about Teddy, she told me she believed that in my engagement with Teddy, I had changed my brain and brain waves. My faith, my intention, and my energy literally effected changes in my brain cells and circuits that enabled me to see the eyes of my teddy bear differently. I began to see him out of a more positive, inclusive cellular construct.

It is what my friend thinks about my experience with Teddy that forms the basis of much of my book, *The Healing of Teddy Bears*: our minds are incredibly powerful, and if they are engaged for positive change, for transformations, we may begin to see ourselves and the world we live in differently. Not only will our perception of the people and world around us undergo a shift, but others will be positively affected by the changing constructs and states of our personal consciousness. So there it is. You and I have the intriguing possibility of transforming ourselves and the world around us by *how* we think and *what* we think.

I don't know why we should have such difficulty believing we can bring about organic changes in our own brains. After all, we already understand, at least vaguely, that if people put too much alcohol or too many drugs into their systems, they can bring about serious chemical-biological changes in their brains and their thinking processes. These organic changes have a profound effect on how a drug-dependent person sees his or her world. The user may well become increasingly suspicious, paranoid and belligerent, all the time believing their perception of reality is accurate. Why should we then not believe that there is a presence within us, and accessible to us, that can effect brain circuit changes that may lead to less egocentricity, more compassion for ourselves and others, and a more hopeful way of seeing the world? How many studies do we need, for example, before we will believe the practice of meditation affects our brains and their circuitry?

I must say, and here my scientifically oriented psychologist friend parts company with me, I see very little difference between the discovery we can influence and change our brains, thereby our perceptions of reality; and, the discovery we can change the molecular structure of stuffed animals and glass eyes.

I believe my imaginative faith created a dialogue with the image of Teddy that my eyes projected. I believe this faith, and the behavior of faith, transformed the makeup of my teddy bear's eyes and body. My reader does not have to accept my adventuresome beliefs, of course, and may believe I am dodging a more likely explanation: projection. But what I am saying is this: if we start with the premise of Mind and its *possibilities*, why should we insist on the *impossibility* of the transformation of matter? As in a teddy bear's glass eyes?

My view curiously resembles stories about Jesus, such his alleged transformation of a poor wine into a really great one during a wedding feast. Miracle stories are often dismissed as common attempts to enhance the stature of various heroes in history by their devotees. Forgive me if I often find myself in the camp of those who are frequently skeptical about the absolute certainties of the skeptics.

I want to be very, very careful how I talk about the "power of the mind." Otherwise the reader and I will be back into the trap of the ego, which wants to suck every spiritual experience and belief into a *power trip*. Perhaps it's better to talk about the power of "Mind," as Hindus do, "Mind" referring to the Life Force, or Being itself, thought of as a non-ego presence. Transforming a stuffed animal's molecular structure from inert energy to live energy is not a parlor trick. Shifting my consciousness from ignoring my teddy bear to affection for my teddy bear was not a parlor trick. No one was around when that event happened, nor would I have been likely to be that expressive with a stuffed animal if anyone had been around, including my wife, who, God knows, is wonderfully accepting of me and all my quirks.

I think if we are to talk about the power within us for transformation, we have to understand power differently than it is ordinarily used. Power often refers to dominance of one kind or another. In this sense it is closely related to our need to control. Power has an association with an aggressive energy, whether the aggression is overt or manipulative. It's of interest that within the Christian tradition Jesus was said to have been tempted to this kind of power by the devil during his wilderness experience. When offered power and glory over all the nations Matthew has him saying, "you will worship and serve only God."

It's useful to think of a different kind of power. It is the softer, less insistent, less conspicuous power within us for transformation, the experience of contemplation rather than acquisition, reflection rather than aggression, silent mind rather noisy mind. Above all, for an understanding of this kind of power, it may prove useful to guide our minds to

our hearts—literally—as a locus for the greatest depths of our consciousness. It is here, in the place of authenticity and compassion that we are somewhat more likely to be liberated from egocentric drives for a self-interested power. I say "somewhat," because the transformation of our minds and attitudes, I think, is seldom as dramatic as my story of a teddy bear. It is much more likely to be incremental, or a victory followed by successive defeats. But the commitment to the deepest within us, I believe that's what the journey is all about.

I don't have much faith that capitalizing "Mind," or "Power" will resolve the human tendency to hunger after spiritual energies for egocentric aims. After all, one does not have to look very far to discover most every spiritual enterprise has been co-opted to damage human beings in horrific ways. But capitalizing the words may at least serve as a reminder great civilizations have believed there is a Life Force inherent in human life and affairs that is eternal and by its nature transformational. Hope, ultimately, is an achievement of the imaginative heart.

CHAPTER 2

The Role of Deconstruction in Transforming Consciousness

*I*n many ways we are familiar with why conscious deconstruction is a necessary requirement for constructive change. An experienced chef tells us that we have a capacity for creative and healthy cooking, but to realize it we'll have to break down the security of our reliance on a familiar list of unhealthy recipes. A tennis coach tells us he realizes we feel secure with how we have learned to serve, but points out we are not likely to reach a higher level of skill and competitiveness unless we change our motion.

I can add many examples of my need to deconstruct ineffectual writing patterns, in favor of forming better ones. You will be able to think of scores of examples when you had to deconstruct a pattern of thinking before you could reconstruct a more successful one, or less self-critical one. In short, the steady transformation of all life forms is both a normal aspect of constructive change, and requires a commitment to the process of deconstruction and construction.

Why should our religious beliefs be exempt from either the evolutionary pull toward constructive shifts of consciousness, or the requirement that we *commit* to the process of deconstruction and reconstruction? To make such a commitment to ourselves and life is to recognize spiritual beliefs are living organisms. We bring the waters of fresh consciousness to them or they begin to shrivel and die. We bring an open heart to them and they give back to us greater enlightenment and joy. These dual functions create a dynamic faith that becomes a steady mountain stream in our lives.

Let me go back now to our first chapter. At one time I'm certain I constructed thought forms that said it would be impossible to affect the material makeup of an inanimate object. In this case a teddy bear. I'm sure I would have believed it to be impossible that I could effect changes in my own brain cells and brain waves, other than through the persistent use of drugs and alcohol. Otherwise, I believed the constitution of the brain was altered only by age and disease. Somewhere along the way I deconstructed these fixed ways of thinking. A process of deconstruction permitted me to construct other forms that were fresher, more flexible, and more comprehensive as to what might be possible. The new forms allowed there could be a *possibility* for finding a depth, or Presence, within myself that *might* be capable of altering my brain and brain waves, a center of energy that *might* be capable of altering the molecular structure of a stuffed animal.

What you may have noticed, in my choice of italicized words in the previous paragraph, is my unwillingness to make a new thought form into a dogmatic promise, into a rule, into a final and fixed thought form. I like to think of the journey of enlarging consciousness as a process, as a scary but creative and joyful exploration of inner space and outer space, of spaces we haven't begun to imagine.

I suggest, as a conscious step in the process of deconstruction-construction, that we focus attention on our hearts and breathing. This may give us a place in our consciousness that provides some objective distance from our persistent and usual thought forms. In Eastern thought, the heart is sometimes described as a sacred energy center, a locus for authenticity, purity, and compassion. This intuited, mythological heart is not identical with one's physical heart, but is part of an invisible, energetic body that underlies our physical body. Whether this energetic heart is a mythological construct, or a mapping of an energetic reality we are just beginning to understand scientifically, makes no difference to me. As a person of faith who is committed to the possible discoveries of inner exploration and experience, I have found that focusing my mind on my heart places my mind at a center for healing and peace that I associate with Being. Such focusing seems to liberate my consciousness from many forms of thought and behavior that are negative, and that limit my appreciation for others and other points of view.

I have occasionally experienced very powerful bursts of visual and somatic recognition that there is an energetic body underlying every human being's physical body. These experiences, the most impressive of which happened unexpectedly during a long meditation retreat with the Buddhist teacher Ruth Denison, created a great sense of awe within me. Cumulatively, such interior experiences have created what I like to think of as a fluid, yet substantial, belief I am one with Being Itself. The One is not separate from us, but inherent as a dynamic presence within all life.

If you are willing to experiment with some interior exploration as we go along, I would like to take you into a short, very short, meditation. Here goes:

Life is. Two words. Monolithic. So intolerable by themselves that our mind rushes to fill the gap. See if this is not so. Say the words, "Life is," with your eyes closed.

Do you not find you want to get on with it, fill the gap—*What* life *is*—Life is *this*, or life is *that*? It is so normal to fill the gaps. Our capacity to reflect on definitions, on names for things, or the meaning of things, seems to define us as human beings, and establishes our differences from trees, plants, birds and animals.

Now, for the moment, see if you can *resist* this ever-so-human tendency to define, put things into boxes. Repeat the same two little words, "Life is," and encourage yourself to resist filling in the gap. Just let the words *be*, on their own. Tolerate an absence of definition and explanations. Tolerate the silence, the emptiness, as it were. If words or definitions come to mind, gently wave them off, as if you were directing traffic. Permit yourself to occupy the silence of being.

I wonder if you felt a moment of awe when your mind quieted? Perhaps some of you might have experienced Mystery, as I did, when I first constructed this experiment. Perhaps it is only my nature, that I would experience Mystery at my core when I feel the full impact of the word *is*. Life *is*. Mystery when I am able to resist defining. This little experiment may illuminate differences in experience, of course, but it also may point to the large part *we* play in our beliefs and how we experience the world. In short, we *participate* in the nature of the reality we create. "Reality" is not just "out there" somewhere, experienced by each of us all the same; inevitably, it is also a *construct*.

Consciously or unconsciously, we have constructed our beliefs about ourselves, the world, and the nature of the universe. One objective of this book is to make explicit the part human beings play in constructing their faith. The body of our beliefs about life and ourselves, or a god for that matter, has not simply been dropped whole onto the earth, and then been shoveled into our minds. In many, many ways, we have helped reconstruct what we have been given. What I hope to encourage in writing this book, is the "fearful delight" of taking full responsibility for our faith. I want to support the courage it requires to be open to a process of deconstructing unexamined beliefs—thought forms—about God, religious icons, morality, traditional religious beliefs, and institutions.

"The deconstruction of unexamined beliefs" is an interesting phrase, because it may so easily be misunderstood, as if the same thought forms need to be deconstructed in every person, and at the same time. But you see, if the transformation of consciousness is a process, then the journey of the soul is an *individualized* process. Not everybody starts at the same place in life, and God knows we are sure different from one another. We can only look to our own hearts to determine what authenticity is asking of *us* at this moment in time. It's impossible to think we all need to deconstruct the same thought forms at identically the same time. How could this possibly be, given our differences, and that we are evolving (I believe) at entirely different rates, often in relationship to the specialized problems we're addressing?

What I am urging, then, is responsibility. Taking responsibility for our own consciousness and change, instead of giving this responsibility to authorities outside ourselves, or comparing ourselves with others. To commit to a consciousness of intention is to empower ourselves. It is a commitment to ground ourselves in the best that we know, the deepest of ourselves, and out of that grounding to create fresh insights and beliefs.

When I did the little "Life is" experiment, I had a difficult time permitting silence. I rushed to fill the gap with abstract words that would put me on firm footing, reassuring me I had "an answer." But my <u>very first</u> experience after I closed my eyes was anxiety. Faced with empty space, I was distressed. That becomes a metaphor, does it not, for how our larger culture, when faced with silence, often feels compelled to fill it? It is not so much that we choose to be on the cell phone, but that one has the feeling many people *have* to be on the cell phone. Without the cell phone, without talking, some people may not know who they are. To hear a voice at the other end of the line reassures them of their own existence.

It is not just the need we may feel to talk. Because of anxiety provoked by silence, we may feel compelled to shop compulsively, eat or drink compulsively, or be sexual compulsively. It is out of terror of the more quiet, softer feelings of intimacy that men or women may rush hurriedly into sex to avoid the scariness of the soft, silent energies of their hearts.

Perhaps we human beings become unbalanced, out of harmony, when we attend to only one or two aspects of ourselves. I like to think there is a time for words, and a time for silence, a time for reflection and a time for action. We need to make room for rational, abstract thinking, but simultaneously develop capabilities for waving off "thinking" in the interests of other aspects of our nature. These other aspects, the intuitive, the creative, our softer feelings, may easily be neglected because they don't give us the same sense of power or control.

To the degree that what I have said previously refers to the thought forms of a religious faith, or a belief system, I want to own how much my own need *for* a faith has contributed to deconstructing certain thought forms and creating others. I did not get to a faith through rational arguments, or become convinced by reason there must be an intelligence behind the universe. No one proved to me life is purposeful. I could always offer up far more convincing arguments that life is stupid and capricious. But I <u>got</u> to a life of faith because I needed faith for my own being to fill, for my imagination to be satisfied. I needed faith to be reassured my creativity would not be shriveled by believing less about myself and the universe than I might. As you see, these are deeply personal and individualistic reasons. I had to create forms of faith that I could experience, not just believe intellectually, and the forms had to work pragmatically. My beliefs had to bring me internal satisfaction and positively affect my relationships with other persons and the world I lived in.

The life and forms of faith will not be the same for many others. For those who feel most comfortable with a "reasonable" faith, and with reasonable methods for arriving at their faith, I have no wish to criticize, particularly if their faith offers them comfort, security, and girds them for a courageous ethical and compassionate life. Nor do I wish to criticize those whose faith is essentially dependent upon an externalized religious system of authority. However, I will speak in later chapters about some of the dangers I believe fixed systems of religious belief pose to an organic, lively faith, and the process of transformation. It may be difficult to commit to the life process of deconstruction and reconstruction if one is overly attached to a fixed religious structure.

This book may be interpreted, then, in its narrower sense, as reflections about faith. I have come to define faith as an intuitive commitment, founded in human longing for a god and for a meaning, lived out at the intersection of the ego and the depths of the heart. But in its larger sense, "Teddy Bears" is an appeal for an awakening of the human spirit to the possibilities for *creating* beliefs about gods, and themselves, that are luminaries of ethical responsibility, joy, and compassion.

CHAPTER 3

Are Spiritual Beliefs Illusions?

*F*reud and Marx believed religion and religious beliefs had no other origin than human beings themselves. In short, there is no transcendent or cosmic being, only wishful thinking it might be so. Marx held religion was merely an "opiate of the people," employed by ancient and contemporary rulers and priests alike to drug the masses into servile, unquestioning obedience and acceptance of their subservient social roles.

Freud believed religious structures and beliefs were created by primitive humans to account for nature's unpredictable power, and by those who have lived after them to provide security in the face of the uncertainties of life and threat of death.

You may be asking, is what Freud said, in particular, so much different from what I wrote in the previous chapter, that we have a capacity as human beings to create our own beliefs about the nature of reality itself? Is there any basic difference between believing the composition of a teddy bear's glass eyes has undergone a transformation and coming to believe there is a God, out of a prior agnosticism? If you have religious beliefs, as I do, are they projections that you have created for the sake of your needs for meaning and security?

Well, yes. Our beliefs must be at the very least, that much, something in which we have participated, a dialogue in which we are engaged. If our human nature, imagination, creativity, and needs for meaning are NOT engaged in the process of an evolving faith, then I think we must have quite a vulgar opinion of the adventuresome curiosity of human beings, our capacity for intelligence and artistic creation. I believe we must not minimize the role human freedom, choice and the initial risk of faith play in any evolution of a dynamic, substantial faith. The process of inner transformation is not simply one of God setting a torch to us like a firecracker so we explode and twirl about earth's backyard of the universe shouting, "I believe, I believe!" Inner transformation is what it suggests about itself, "Inner," for the most part, not ordinarily observable, incremental. Which is not to say we may not, from time to time, have rare moments of real drama and surprise, when we are convinced external signs of The Divine Presence are presenting themselves to us. But my point at the moment is that we are competent to participate in the human formulation-dissolution-formulation-dissolution dynamic of faith and inner transformation. Later on I will re-visit the theme of external signs and the role they play in some of us becoming persons of faith.

It is unwise, and even evasive in my opinion, to minimize our personal responsibility for reflection, creativity and complexity in the evolution of our personal faith. To address the issue of faith any other way is to make someone, or some other being, responsible for it, and to see our role as largely one of obedience to a system, a person, or other being, rather than fidelity to our inner witness.

Where we part company with Freud and Marx is in our affirmation of the timeless Presence of Being, what we believe and/or experience to be a spiritual reality permeating all of creation, from uncounted universes to our very own body cells and minds. English translations of Hindu writings invariably capitalize Mind when they refer to this Divine Presence which permeates all, including mind, or human intelligence, spelled with a small "m."

It may be helpful, as you think about your own thought process in reading this book, or reflecting upon it, to think of Being, which is sometimes called "God," as Timeless Presence. While it might be awkward, if not strange, to converse with anyone about God as "Timeless Presence," I am suggesting there is some advantage in being able to go inside our minds and bodies through our consciousness, simply breathe in and out, and be open to the possible experience of "Timeless Presence."

If one is beginning an inner exploration, a prior mental image as to what "God," might mean may block fresh visualizations. It is best to let go of whatever familiar thoughts or images pass through our minds, and simply experience our breathing up into our brains and hearts, and then back out, into our solar plexus and extremities.

To become one with our breathing aids our consciousness in "becoming the one who notices," the part not identified with our egos and repetitive thinking. Focusing on our breathing cultivates a skill that helps us connect peacefulness with silence. It also helps us understand what an "observing mind" might be, one which observes the mind but does not identify with its obsessions, observes our critical nature or skepticism, but is not consumed by it. Such experiments, or explorations if you will, constitute a science of the inner life.

While our egos and our rational-critical minds are not well-equipped for inner journeys, our hearts and our intuitive minds are. It is the intuitive part of our brain that is more likely to be able to experience Presence unbound by space and time. And it is the heart which is able to give itself up to this Presence in love and joy, to feel a union with Being Itself which is peaceful and relaxing. Some writers believe this moment, or successions of moments, is when the human soul is truly at home with its origin and destiny. Other writers have suggested when such moments are constant in human consciousness, we have our best description of what it means to be a self-realized being.

To be a person of faith, in my view, is to be internally, and intentionally, a more conscious being. It is like awakening to find you had a friend you did not know you had, or a lover. The sudden realization one has faith is sometimes called "awakening." Early Christians saw it as even more radical than awakening. They called it a deliverance from death into life, and symbolized the process in the act of baptism. They believed Jesus' resurrection was the forerunner and symbol of their own resurrection from spiritual deadness, and ultimately the forerunner of their own victory over human mortality.

The path I have described, based on experience and inner consciousness, could be called mysticism, and I will devote more time to this path to faith in a future chapter. For now I would like to return to an allusion I made earlier, that some persons come to faith through "happenings," or events outside themselves. These are occurrences so arresting, those experiencing them believe they are a revelation, a manifestation of The Divine, a Voice from a different dimension than our own.

Judaic and Christian scriptures are full of these unexpected, often dramatic, "revelations of God." The pages of this book could be filled with such stories from every religious tradition. Or, they could be filled with stories submitted by readers who initially came to a faith in The Divine through unexpected, even startling, events in their lives.

Let me allude briefly to my experience with "revelation," a dawning conviction I was hearing the Voice from another dimension than my familiar one. My familiar one was agnosticism. Not religious myself by background, or pre-disposed to faith, I nevertheless was curious about the reasons why various friends of mine attended services on Saturdays or Sundays. On rare occasions I wondered, if there were a God, how would one find out? True to my nature, I suppose, I never was tempted to believe I could reason my way to a faith. After all, there were as many "reasons" to believe it was impossible to believe there could be a god as there were there must be a god. I do recall asking myself one day, as I helped my father mix and spread cement for a walkway, if we were to come back in another lifetime, would we do it as a lizard, or a dog?

I was not what one would call a thoughtful agnostic. I did not come to such a position by hard mental and emotional work. I came by it more naturally, growing up in a home where religion was never discussed, never even mentioned, neither favorably nor negatively. I was, then, an ignorant agnostic, and a mostly uncurious one, other than the day we mixed cement.

Nor did I ask any serious religious questions when I was an army paratrooper. Why I should have become curious about religion after I was discharged, and prepared to go on to college, is also an unknown. Perhaps now that the survival issues of a war were behind me, and my parents were successfully divorced, their property divided, I felt some liberty of mind to become curious about larger things than immediate survival.

But how to go about satisfying this curiosity? There were churches, of course, and I could attend a few services. So I did that, dragging along a laboring man who worked for my father so I would not feel so strange in such an environment. I think we went twice, and the experience was unmemorable, so we stopped. One could say my curiosity was somewhat shallow, or the services lacked whatever vitality we expected. In any event, my next thought was books. So I went to the library and chose two books that were contemporary and promised to talk about religion. One caught my attention because I spent some time with the words of Jesus in the Gospel of Matthew, neither of which I knew anything about. The author, Emmett Fox, interpreted the contemporary meaning of The Sermon on the Mount, and I found that interesting. The other book was well beyond my capabilities and held no interest for me at all.

Ultimately I decided there had to be a more direct way to finding out if there was a god or not than by reading books or going to church services. If there was a god, was it not likely that god might communicate with me directly? With that in mind I determined to conduct my own simple experiment. I would go inside. I had heard about prayer of course, but never prayed, or been tempted to pray. But I did suppose, if there were a god, to pray directly to such a possible Being was a likely way to go. So I prayed, very simply and directly: "If you exist, show me in some way you do exist." And that was it. From there I went about whatever business was at hand, though I often had the prayer in the background of my mind in whatever I was doing.

I was at an in-between place, out of the army, but not having yet started college because I had to wait for a new semester. A good time to travel to northern California to visit my mother and stepfather, whom I had not seen for two years. During my visit we all went to see a movie, "The Razor's Edge," a screen adaptation of a book by Somerset Maugham. The chief character, played by Tyrone Power, found himself dissatisfied with his wealthy and profligate life and made a trip to India. During his stay he came to study with a spiritual teacher, began to meditate, and had subsequent inner experiences which were so full of light he became a person of faith. But it was not just that he came into an awe he had never experienced before, it was that his belief in a Divine Being also convinced him he needed to lead a life of purpose. He returned home, no longer drinking heavily, and expressed great compassion for his former circle of wealthy friends, whom he recognized to be continuing on, unfulfilled and unhappy as he had been. Affected by his peacefulness, some of his friends, too, began search for deeper meaning in their lives.

This film made a profound impression on me. Though younger than the lead character, and certainly not wealthy, I realized I wanted my life to have far more meaning than it did. I began to see that a mentality of searching and faith could result in a life of purpose, comprehending human existence as purposeful. One might say I connected my prayer—if there was a God, would He reveal Himself to me in some undeniable way—with my awakening while watching this film. I was awakened to a longing for my life to have purpose and simultaneously stirred to believe it was no less than God Himself Who was shaking me by the shoulder as I lay asleep.

Stunned by my experience, all the way home on the train I reflected on what could have happened. I read more of both books from the library, which I had taken on the trip, but particularly from the Emmett Fox.

A few weeks later I met a young man my age on the basketball court at the college I had begun to attend. He was a terrific player, a center. I was a guard, and we made a good team. Doug invited me to attend his church with him and have dinner with his family afterward, and I welcomed the opportunity. The second Sunday I attended their worship service the pastor read from the exact selection in the Book of Matthew, chapter and verses, I had particularly attended to in the Emmett Fox book. I was in awe. Increasingly it seemed to me, God was revealing Himself to me. I was becoming a believer because a variety of circumstances were converging in ways I found undeniable in establishing God as the fundamental Mover and reality of the universe. Within less than a year I had come not only to a faith, but to believe it was my destiny to become a minister.

I don't have any trouble believing the God who created uncounted universes is also the God of history, both *of* our history and *not* of our history. His Being, in my view, is by its very nature inter-penetrating of all that is. Why should I doubt He would be interested in our petty little struggles? Why should I doubt that the One who created the universes, is also the One fully capable and intelligent as to how He intervenes in the events and experiences of our world? Yes, even our tiny psyches!

Are arresting events embedded in life and history for all persons, for anyone to come to faith that way? Yes, I believe so. But I also think we must have an open mind and heart, and be capable of a kind of innocence. We have to have some capacity to give as much weight to our innocence and longings as we give weight to our skepticism and "reasons" for disbelief. Some people are lopsided.

A father and his son once attended a parade that announced the arrival of a circus in the town. The young son, who had never seen a parade before, was very excited. He had an image that many exciting performers and animals would pass by him, but there would be one that would surpass them all. His father had told him, in fact, that he should watch carefully, because there was one thing that would pass by he would never, ever, forget. He could not wait to see this special "thing" arrive, and he wondered if he would faint because of excitement. As it happened, a band passed playing loudly, swinging trombones and trumpets back and forth in the sun. But while impressive, the little boy thought this was not the special thing. He did not feel close to fainting. Then cages with lions passed by, pacing back and forth. That was not it either. The elephants came next, their trunks sweeping one way and then the other, little men or women on top of them holding reins. After the elephants, beautiful horses with pretty young girls standing on top of them. There were huge strong men, with bulging muscles, there were clowns throwing balls in the air and catching them, coming close and grinning at him. And so on it went, one act after another, acrobats, zebras, tigers and monkeys. Then the parade was over, gone.

The little boy looked up at his father, who was holding his hand.

"Daddy, where is the special thing, the one you told me about that was so big?"

The father looked down at his son. "You didn't see it? You didn't see the elephants, how huge they were? How did you miss them?"

Sometimes the issue of faith is like this. We carry such unusual expectations in our minds as to what God is supposed to "look like" that we miss the elephant when it passes. I am suggesting it is likely all of us have experiences in our lifetimes that initiate a sense of wonderment and awe. But instead of taking a step to surrender our hearts to these moving interior experiences, we find reasons to forget or otherwise minimize them. We become skeptical that what we have just experienced is "the thing." We wait for the next act to pass, after the elephants have gone by.

To return, once again, to the mystical way some persons arrive at faith, let us see how these two paths of revelation, and the need to create faith, merge. It was surely out of curiosity I made my first prayer, that if there was a God, show me. But was it not, also, because of my human need for larger meaning in my life, that I was receptive to a film about a man who *finds* meaning?

In many ways we cooperate in creating the conditions of faith. I took some religious books out from the library. One of those books had a pragmatic impact because it spoke of everyday issues relevant to me. I like to think that I was arranging some pieces of what would become my history. I was playing my part in organizing my consciousness to be receptive to a pattern of events as they fell into place, culminating not only in a conviction there was a God, but that He had a purpose for my life.

Do I also believe in Providence, that there were mysterious goings-on too coincidental to account for them as mere accidents or fate? Yes, I do. I believe there was a Divine Presence affecting, putting some weight, to these events.

I believe faith is a gift of Grace. But I also believe faith requires a certain curiosity, innocence and capacity for awe, to be fully birthed. Just as it takes a sperm and an egg to bring about life, so it is both the Presence of the Divine and the open response of a human that together generate faith.

CHAPTER 4

Our Human Need for Authority

We generally acknowledge human beings have needs for survival, such as adequate food, protection from the elements, treatment of illness and injuries, and nurturance in our earliest years. To the degree survival needs are met, we are more contented and less stressed. To the degree our needs are threatened or not met, we are more subject to anxiety and fear. As fear increases the human tendency is to withdraw or become increasingly angry.

The role of authority is to provide social structures for well-being and survival, and verbal assurances that will reduce anxiety and fear. History has taught us that competition among nations, resulting in the most terrible of wars and suffering, has originated time and again from two sources: the fear of nations that their very survival is at stake, and the use or misuse of power by those in authority.

It is not my intention to address, more than I have, the absolutely gargantuan social issues connected to the human fear of death and the role of authority in allaying such fears by providing security. Still, as must be self-evident, the threat of further terrorism in our country in recent years resulted in greater reliance on our military, and greater power vested in Presidential authority by a sizable proportion of our citizens. Nor should it pass without notice that many political leaders are not beyond appealing to the fear of terrorism in an intentional, if not utterly cynical, pitch to get elected.

My preoccupation in this chapter will be with religious authority and its role in addressing the fear of mortality and the need to believe it is possible after death to go to a "haven of rest." Of course, it is obvious the fear of death and the aftermath of death are on the same continuum, so church and state have, in many ways, been about the same business historically of providing structures and reassurances that will reduce fear on the basis of the authority of civil and religious pronouncements.

Given that our lives are made infinitely easier by civil laws and expectations established and enforced by authority, down to such a simple thing as a traffic light, is it not true we need authority for our moral and spiritual life? Do we have a socially equivalent need in our spirits for religious authority? Does it make life easier and less anxious to turn to a religious tradition, a set of religious writings, a person of authority, to give us a structure for how to live? Do we not need a voice of authority which will reassure us in contending with what may be our greatest fear of all, dying and the aftermath of death?

The answer is, yes, yes it *is* easier to turn to authority somewhere for wisdom and guidance. And yes, at the very least, it *is* so very human to long for a voice of authority to reassure us about death and its aftermath. In fact, most of us have initiated a spiritual journey by turning to the most valued voices available when we first commenced our spiritual search.

Those sources may range from the religion of our parents to courses in Judaism, Christian thought, Islamic history and tradition, to far ranging studies of eastern religions, or more esoteric writings. We may read books that challenge our assumptions, or begin biblical studies, or hear of a teacher of spiritual power and ethical influence. One has to begin somewhere when starting a spiritual journey, just as one starts with parents when beginning the journey of life. Parents are our earliest authorities for how to grow up well.

But having acknowledged our initial need for externalized authority, in growing up socially or ethically and spiritually, I think it is worth looking at some of the dangers of too heavy a reliance on external authority. The largest danger is in what we may long for most, a voice of authority that is absolute, a commanding voice that sways our emotions and captivates our idealism.

For those of you who have a religious background, I encourage you to keep your heart open to the entire flow of wisdom, guidance and love you have received from your history. At the same time, see if you can let go, as if you were releasing the pressure of a hand-grip on a steering wheel, let go of any mental insistence your treasured tradition must be preserved as absolute. By absolute I mean, under any and all circumstances, eternal and timeless in its validity. By absolute I mean, for you it is not open to any kind of doubt or question, even about the smallest piece of its authority. By absolute I mean you might feel guilty or frightened should you bring any part of your tradition into question. Your security might seem to you to be at stake; and, indeed, if your security is attached to a perception that only your tradition is absolute, none other, then it *is* at stake if you ask serious questions of it.

I would like to believe my readers will be able to maintain an appreciation for their historical beliefs, and the beliefs of those of many other differing traditions, and at the same time be able to bring into visibility the danger of vesting any tradition, institution, or person with absolute authority.

We are familiar with what has happened with Muslim fundamentalism, far too many teachers of Islam preaching hate and supporting violence. Devotees of fundamentalist Islam such as Bin Laden announce with passion and self-righteousness that it is their intention to extinguish capitalism through whatever deaths are required, however many innocents. But we must recognize a similar polarization occurs within all religious traditions, including Judaism and Christianity, wherever sacred writings are held to be of absolute origin and unquestioning validity. Jewish fundamentalists, too, function from what they consider to be a biblical mandate, to possess the entirety of ancient Israel even as they anticipate the return of a messiah, and their willingness to die for their cause.

Many Christian fundamentalists are equally possessed of a belief God has chosen them alone to be saved through Jesus Christ, and no others, and that the Bible is a mandate for absolute beliefs, rigidity of thought and behavior. Are Papal fundamentalists very far behind in their belief the Pope always speaks with the authority of God and all else is heresy?

My own crises of faith-absolutism could be highlighted in two incidents. In what seems by now almost an entirely different lifetime, I was a committed fundamentalist Christian who devoted countless hours acquiring and reading books devoted to biblical infallibility. Fortunately I was not limited to listening to voices outside myself. I also was persuaded by troubles of my own nature to pursue an inward path, searching my moral soul and heart for self-understanding. Eventually these two intense vehicles of learning, faith-absolutism and my heart, met at intersections where a collision was inevitable.

I had been a Christian minister for several years when I joined the local Ministerial Association, comprised of pastors from various churches in my California community. Over time I came to respect the integrity and spirit of each minister, including three whose churches would be called mainline protestant. Of the three, one pastor in particular disturbed me. He rocked my boat, not only through his broad intelligence, but because he stood out as a person of deep compassion. But he was not "of the faith," meaning the faith I had been told saved people. His position in decisions we made frequently reflected strong ethical convictions that seemed disconnected from harsh judgment, and inseparable from compassion and discernment about the complexity of the many issues we had to consider. I was forced to look at my own tendency to react to these issues moralistically, in oversimplified ways, often self-advancing ways.

I think I had been living in a fairly contained box of beliefs I had been taught in Bible College, the reassuring message of my own preaching, and my fairly exclusive social affiliation with my own "kind." My exposure to a broad range of pastoral leadership and more liberal belief systems posed a threat to the security system which reassured me God loved me, and that I was among the "saved." My belief system, what I had been taught and apparently needed for my security, was quite simple: I, as an evangelical Christian, was "saved," and these other folk, "liberals," were not.

How was I to deal with this crisis? According to my authority system, this man who troubled my soul was damned eternally, shut out of the Kingdom of God. Yet, he was a person I admired for his goodness. According to my heart, he belonged to God as fully as I. My trained mind and my heart were on a collision course. It was my heart that broke through the crust of my "faith." If this man, who was good, honest and compassionate, could not be in the Kingdom of God because he did not believe as I, then how was it I could POSSIBLY be in the Kingdom of God, knowing what I did about myself? How many of my attitudes were oversimplifications, refusals to take into account the ambiguous character of an issue? How much of the time did my own ego play a very large role in my perspective, when a community "moral" issue was under consideration by our ministerial association?

There seemed to be no other way to put it: if this man did not deserve to be in the Kingdom of God because he did not belong to the true church, or practice immersion for baptism, then the God of such a Kingdom was not the kind of God I would choose to believe in.

I had not yet settled for myself the underlying issue of authority, in this case biblical infallibility, which would ultimately prove to be crucial. My "denomination," though it claimed to be non-denominational, was founded on separatist beliefs based on certain biblical passages. The biblical passages, in turn, were considered infallible guides to truth. But I *had* decided the existential issue, of who God would have to be, if I were to have a God. It would be a God of compassion and inclusiveness, not one of division, suspicion and tribal superiority. It would be the God of Mystery, not the God of black and white oversimplification, separating the saved from the unsaved. It was these two systems, separatism and inclusiveness, that came into conflict in my beliefs and practices.

The second major threat to my religious security system came about in the first year of my study for a second theological degree, from a seminary where neither its professors nor its students were expected to subscribe unquestioningly to a belief in biblical infallibility. I remember the night I experienced my spiritual crisis, in front of the fireplace of our New England parsonage. I had shuffled out to where my wife sat, after our four children were in bed and asleep. She looked up at me, realizing I looked pale and apparently stunned. "What's wrong?" she asked.

"I don't know if I believe in God anymore," I weakly replied.

If she was shaken, she did not show it. If anything, she looked compassionate. It was unusual for me to show what might be considered weaknesses, or express any sense of disappointment or loss. She was aware I was very vulnerable at the moment, and sharing something with her of untold importance, around which I had centered much of my adult life.

That evening we were very close. The fire warmed us. Usually not at a loss for words, I had little to say. She valued the silence as a time of accepting what I was experiencing as a traumatic loss, and a core of what had constituted so much of my identity. We sat in silence for a long period of time, until she hugged me and told me she was so sorry I was going through such pain. Then we went to bed, since it was close to midnight, and I continued to be in something of a daze, but very determined I would not flee from either my loss or the shock. I had some true notion in my own heart that a necessary process was occurring. I even had a strange kind of confidence that I was experiencing a quite necessary loss of a certain kind of faith. I had lost an imprisoned concept of God. Nevertheless, I believed the God who had revealed His reality to me two decades earlier, and who had brought me to New England to go to school, the larger God of consciousness, had not abandoned me. Then I went to sleep.

Next morning I awakened to God. What I mean is, when I woke up I had this surging sense of God within me. What I had lost was a previously unrecognized way I had come to identify the existence and nature of God with biblical infallibility. If one went, the other would be gone, too, such was the nature of my unconscious linking of one to the other. Gone was my investment in the absolute authority of scripture as infallible. Still vibrant and present was my internal experience of the reality of God.

So what about our needs for a security system, a reliable structure of authority? Where shall we go for the truth about how to live, what is to happen to us after we die, the truth about what constitutes metaphysical reality? Where will we go to find God Himself?

Within. We learn to journey into inner space. But here, too, we must be cautious. We must hold up similar warning signs about assigning absolute truth, absolute reality, to what we discover in our inward journey of faith. Have there not been many persons in history who "went inside," and concluded they were God's messengers? And yet the messages from these persons who have gone inside frequently contradict one another, and also are at variance with more ancient and treasured traditions of sacred writings. Every day we hear of people who "trusted their own counsel," and were led to write diatribes of hate, or who did violence to others. Not all people make claims crazy enough for them to be hospitalized. Some of them preach visions of hate which threaten our very existence as a civilization, even as they are thought of as role models and heroes, rather than possessed.

It is not enough to bring into question external claims to absolute authority. We must also be willing to bring into question perceptions and beliefs we arrive at internally. We must test out perceptions and beliefs, no matter how powerful or stirring they might be, no matter how certain we feel at the time, with our hearts. We must test them out from the vantage point of the wisdom of spiritual teachers known for their integrity and compassion. And above all, we must be reluctant to identify our egos with our beliefs, so we are not fixated on the notion of absolute knowledge, any unquestioning assumption we have "arrived at *the* truth."

Truth, experienced in our own depths, has a paradoxical character of being simultaneously commanding and powerful, yet at the same time ephemeral, as if it could drift away in the next moment. My heart tells me this is so, truth is a visitation of consciousness, a gift, and we are to respond to it wisely and in the moment. But the next moment is the next moment, and who knows what gifts God may have for us, what powerful truths lie in wait for us in the next moment?

Sometimes people think they will escape the limitations of their parents' type of scriptural or institutional faith by a fresh approach, studying with a teacher, a guru. They like to believe they can shed stale teachings from their history as they would a sweater they think to be out of style. But I would encourage caution, caution, caution, in trusting the "insights" of anyone who makes claims too easily about their enlightenment. I might even dare to suggest running in the other direction, especially if they exhibit an arrogant intolerance of your own beliefs.

My prejudice is that both a teacher and any student may be taken in by a mutually shared hypnotic belief system that all moral and spiritual truth originates with a single "enlightened being." How often have we read of spiritual teachers gathering a flock of charmed people, men and women, young and old, and eventually leading them into behaviors hostile and destructive to their families, their society, and themselves? And how often have "disciples" been asked to sell their possessions and turn the proceeds over to the teacher's organization, supposedly in order to free the disciples from attachments that could be a hindrance to their spiritual advancement?

We find ourselves amazed that people can become so persuaded of "truths" they have found, and the absolute reliability of a teacher's authority, that they have become willing to commit shameful, immoral acts, including attempting to kill authorities who might be investigating such cults or communes. We find it astounding sometimes that disciples are willing to kill or die for their "teacher," or at the very least sell all that they possess. These are not simply ignorant and poverty-stricken people. More often than not they are well-educated, spiritually motivated and intelligent. But something has happened to cause them to leave their brains and critical faculties of faith at the door of the compound, or to turn them over to the teacher when he or she asks it.

I am attempting to give some backdrop, to establish how considerable the human need appears to be to believe there *is* such a thing as "Absolute Truth," and how great the need for dependency on those who make such claims. It is frightening how much people are willing to give up of their own nature, their basic autonomy, and a trust of their own moral instincts. Is this because of a human tendency to be frightened, even terrified, of what has been called our existential loneliness in the universe? That we flee from a terror of our basic aloneness by seeking rescue from a person or system that offers us security?

Many years ago I would sometimes read of a spiritual teacher by the name of Bubba Free John, who had a huge following in the San Francisco Bay area. Then one day I heard from one of his students that he had withdrawn from his followers. It seems he no longer wanted to sustain a system that, in his view, promoted spiritual dependency. Apparently he saw clearly where this tremendous abundance of energy invested in him as an authoritative teacher of enlightenment was headed. He had come to believe such a structure created transformational dwarfism. So he refused to play the role and, in effect, publicly disappeared, became anonymous. He managed to escape the hypnotic spell that frequently traps spiritual "teachers" and students drawn to charismatic teachers.

It has been 30 years or more, and I don't know what has happened since to Bubba Free John or his original disciples. Did his former students "grow up," and take responsibility for their own faith and its evolution? I don't know. But I have not forgotten the story, and I admire Free John's alleged intention to defuse the powerful energies of dependency. It is a parabolic warning about the dangers of any claim to absolute authority.

CHAPTER 5

Spirituality as a Process

The journey of personal transformation may best be seen as a *process*, an evolution of faith and consciousness that is life-long. But it too often is viewed as a building project: building up faith, or building a permanent structure of beliefs. At other times faith is thought of as something one subscribes to, and adopts by moving into a house of beliefs previously constructed by a charismatic figure or an institutional authority. How does this shift from a personal, individualistic faith to an abstract structure of beliefs occur? I think less from the need for an institution to impose its system of authority and conformity on its adherents, and more from a natural human tendency to substitute dependency for responsibility. It is simply more secure to shift from the awesome, often lonely, responsibility for personal faith to a well-defined set of beliefs determined by a religious institution or charismatic arrogance.

While many members of authoritative religious institutions *do* maintain a vital personal faith and a strong sense of individual responsibility for their faith and behavior, it is often because they are at odds with their institution. They are privately at odds with authority, and simply go on evolving their own faith and private views, despite what the institution or its leaders declare. Unfortunately, a more common tendency in systems based on authority is toward unthinking and unquestioning identification with a particular faith-blueprint. Biblical inerrancy and infallibility are to be *defended*, not explored. A charismatic teacher who lays claims to absolute truth is to be *idealized* and given cultic power, rather subjected to honest doubts and questions.. A Church based on the claim to infallibility through apostolic succession is given the kind of seductive power that parishioners encourage because of their fears and cultural familiarity.

Cultivating faith in an institution, or charismatic person, and structuring faith along the lines of what authority figures declare to be absolute, does create a lot of energy. But it is not the energy of a personal, highly individualistic faith. It is the energy of projected ego-identification with systems of belief, or persons who lay claim to absolute wisdom. It is tribal energy, loyalty to one's tribe and what its elders teach. The very exclusiveness of a tribe gives its members an identity. And when institutions or authoritative figures make claims for absolute truth, those who believe the pronouncements take on an additional, exclusive, energetic charge: they and the tribe *know*, and those from other tribes *don't* know. Those in the tribe belong to God, or have eternal promise, and those in other tribes don't belong to God or have eternal promise.

It is not that all individual members of such institutions believe in such divisive and damaging exclusiveness. Many have hearts that are larger than their programmed thinking. And, as I have said, some have a private faith that is at odds with what their own institution believes about having a corner on eternal truth.

I find that as I write I want to point out: while there is a condition of spiritual dependency that is deadly to a lively, organic faith, there is always within each of us a countering spirit, though sometimes buried deeply and out of sight, that *wants* to create a hard-won personal faith. So while I believe the tendency within systems based on biblical or church authority is to create dependency, conformity of beliefs, and arrested faith, I must add that some persons within those settings manage to create their own faith and walk their own path. They may appreciate their institutional environment for a variety of reasons, but they simultaneously keep their own counsel.

What does it mean if we describe spirituality and faith as a *process*, rather than a project? It means spirituality is a state of consciousness that must be fed and cultivated, and it means faith is a changing, live organism. It means we have something to do with the faith we have. We are in part its creator. Vital faith is a malleable passion of the heart for truth, authenticity and compassion. A vital faith is one that continues to create fresh visions of spiritual reality.

The struggle between authoritative systems and spirituality as process has always been present, but appears to be generating more fire at the moment. As I write this chapter this morning, I read of the present pope's denunciation of two books, both written by priest-scholars from different orders. The books independently theorized that stories Mary was a virgin when Jesus was born had no validity in historical reality, but were added later by writers to support claims by Christians that Jesus was Divine. Virgin birth stories were extant in other mid-eastern mythologies, and scholars believe they were attached to religious and political personalities to magnify their claim to divine authority.

It's obvious that two systems of absolute authority were threatened by what the scholar-priests wrote when they questioned the virgin birth: biblical infallibility and papal infallibility. The pope had no choice but to denounce these writers. He commands the castle and is responsible for the faith of all who live within its boundaries. He *must* fire away from the ramparts of Rome, just as some popes have attacked scientists in the past and participated in the execution of dissenters from the faith, as defined by The Holy Roman Church.

Having suggested that a faith based upon authority has a tendency to be more intellectual, static, and contained, I would like to devote more space toward viewing faith as a process.

My personal faith, I believe, is all the more inclusive, organic and unpredictable because of many religious traditions feeding into it. That, and because of varied and powerful life experiences over more than 70 years of living. Of all the religious traditions from which I have been nurtured, the two most influential ones have been that of Jesus and the Apostle Paul, and Buddhist Vipassana meditation.

You may have heard of a circle of biblical experts called "The Jesus Scholars." These are teachers from a wide range of universities and seminaries who meet regularly to examine the New Testament, and more specifically the four Gospels. They also look into religious and historical writings of the same period that are not in the biblical canon. They compare oldest copies of original documents, and attempt to identify what must have been at first similar oral traditions about the teachings and life of Jesus. Their goal is to determine, as much as it might be possible, what Jesus said and did, as over against words and actions that were likely imposed on his history at a later date.

First, let it be said, those who believe the Bible is inerrant and infallible will feel obliged to defend that faith. They will believe the Jesus

Scholars are the enemy, an abomination to be attacked because they are bringing into question "the blueprint." concept of faith

My reservations about the Jesus Scholar efforts are somewhat different. I am afraid the attempt to establish historical authenticity for some of what Jesus did and taught, will simply create another possibility for a "reliable" source of authority. There may be a tendency to see what is left after the scholars get finished as "the truth" for a life of faith. Not that it would be what the Jesus Scholars had in mind, but simply as an outcome of the human tendency to want a reliable authority to affix their faith. The bones that remain may still be treated as venerable in a way that would make me uneasy. Having expressed my reservations, it is still the case, as a matter of intellectual curiosity, that I am very interested in what the Jesus scholars are about. I suspect when they have completed "their" canon, I will still find myself inspired by some sayings and actions of Jesus that they have decided were *later* accretions, less likely to be the actual historical words and actions of Jesus.

If faith is a process, which I believe it is, I like the idea of reading the Gospels without having to worry about whether this incident or that incident "really happened." I like considering the Gospel record of Jesus' teachings for what they are, and not having to consult "Jesus Scholar" books to discover which of his teachings are likely to have been uttered by the real person, and which are more likely to have been added from classical traditions at a later date.

Take one small example. It is said Jesus taught, "Knock and the door shall be opened. Ask and you will receive." This is truth for me. It is a statement about what it means to open our hearts. It is a statement about how the universe behaves under certain conditions. It is a statement about prayer, and the responsiveness of Being Itself, under certain conditions. Confidence in such a teaching is core to my faith. Does it help to think Jesus, himself, probably said it? Maybe. I like to visualize Jesus saying it. But I believe the sentiment of the words because they accord with my nature, with my needs and longings. My faith inclines toward the highly anthropomorphic, toward the personal rather than intellectual and scientific, toward a sense of the inherence of Being in human affairs, rather than transcendence. For a person of dynamic faith, differently psychically composed, the words, "knock and the door shall be opened," may create no energetic charge at all. Perhaps something else, other words, will create a confirming charge.

If spirituality is a process, then we must be open to how unique faith is to each *person*, how an alive, dynamic faith always interacts mutually with the specific nature of a person having and wanting such a faith. My genetic structure, how I am put together, how I was shaped by my history, who has entered my life, what kinds of gifts I have been given, what kind of suffering I have experienced: all of these and far more comprise my "nature." My nature plays an important role in the kind of faith I have, and the kind of faith I need.

Go back to the simple words, "Ask and you will receive." How faith takes those words in, interprets them, lives them out, I don't think is simple at all. It is as complex as being able to tolerate a certain open-endedness in believing the universe will respond to our asking for what we need, or what others need. It is as complex as being able to tolerate silence, Divine withholding, paradox, and doubt. It is as complex as our capacity for rationalization and imaginative creating. It is about a kind of innocence, the delights of intentional naivety, giving up requirements for absolute certainty and proof.

If you say to me that I am making up my faith as I go along, I would say you are right. And not only are you right, but you have hit upon the main thrust of this book, that I believe *everyone* creates his own faith. My only interest is whether or not the faith people are creating is worthy of them, worthy of their best creative, imaginative efforts. *Is the god that we create worthy of becoming the God who can create us?* By that I mean, a God who can mold us into beings of courage, authenticity and compassion.

My interest in illuminating how we creatively form our faith objects and beliefs is to encourage spiritual creativity as a *conscious* behavior. I encourage people to take responsibility for the creation of their personal faith because I don't think we should give that responsibility to authority figures. Why shouldn't *we* experience the delight and joy of a faith we create? I trust that human beings are capable of overcoming their fear of themselves and the loss of authority figures in spiritual matters.

A scholar by the name of Emil Brunner once said, "The Gospel is self-authenticating." By that he meant that to hear it was to be persuaded of the power and truth of its message. I believe when we hear some great spiritual teachers, or when we read from honored spiritual traditions, if we have open hearts we may be energetically affected by some teachings, and elements of some traditions. These become part of the clay we need to mould our personal faith. They are the words that have potency for us, that stir up a congruent energy that "speaks" to us. At this point, what you take in becomes part of a life process in formulating your faith. You have a dialogue with the universe.

In one sense the spiritual journey is not so hard as it looks. It is a matter of recognizing we have a spiritual longing, and then being open to life as it comes to us so we engage it for learning. This learning can occur anywhere; any time. *How* we formulate our faith may depend on one simple, unexpected act of kindness toward us. So it is not just who we learn from, it is what we learn, and how open we are to being taught by the universe so that we can take it in, integrate it into a vital faith consciousness.

The key phrase to remember is that a "happening" must resonate with our own being. It is how the universe speaks to *our* nature, not someone else, even if that someone else is our husband or one of our children. How can we have a faith that we participate in, that we help create, unless we recognize we are constantly being given the materials from the universe for creating faith? We have to find out where the surges of energy come from in our lives. From what religious tradition, what teacher, what relationship, what activity, what moral demand. And where the surge of energy is, there will be where you will find the universe speaking to you, offering you the "revelations" you need to form a dynamic, healing faith.

Once we understand faith is a process it is easier to understand why no one has ever been able to resolve the question of whether faith is a gift or a spiritual attitude. Faith is both. To initiate a journey of faith one must be possessed of a certain kind of innocence. It's hard to question our own set formulations if we think we know everything. One could refer to mind-innocence as an openness of heart. Some persons in the faith journey have contended they had no faith at all until they were jolted out of their certainties. Powerful and unexpected events broke them open. They became accessible to a faith consciousness. It's understandable why they would think of faith as a gift. I, too, think of faith as a gift of God's grace; in short, that I would not have a faith at all if some quite strange events had not occurred in the 19th year of my life, prompting me to ask probing questions, and to become a more conscious seeker and creator of my faith.

So far, I have said I believe spirituality is understood at its best as a process that includes an ongoing dialogue between our consciousness and universal reality, whether the primary initiative is seen as originating with Being Itself, or in human need and curiosity. I have suggested the shape of our faith will likely be consistent with our particular and individual natures. While you and I may have some general agreement about the value of faith in our lives, how we *experience* faith, and how we experience and describe the *object*(s) of our faith, may vary considerably.

A real question is, do we want a faith that welcomes questions and paradox and often leads to an enlargement of our consciousness and greater generosity of spirit? Or, will we settle for a faith that veers toward polarization: us against them, truth against falsehood, good against evil? The tendency to be defensive, to occupy a fortress mentality, is not exclusively a fundamentalist trap. Unfortunately, many so-called "liberal" faiths seem equally at home with a fortress mentality, lobbing arrows of verbal hostility from their crossbows toward those who hold a more conservative faith. Our faith does not require us to judge others harshly, or to distance ourselves from those who differ from us, but to be clear about humanely harmful excesses possible to *any* faith. And I would, of course, include atheism and agnosticism as systems of faith subject to their own excesses.

After a very satisfying Thai dinner with friends one evening, we unexpectedly got into a discussion of "deeper things" on our way home. Our friend said she thought the arousal of faith began with a longing for meaning. We could not complete our conversation that evening, but I reflected on her comment lengthily after I got home, and later sent an email with my further thoughts.

Yes, we do have something to do with the faith we end up having. It is indeed possible we "create" objects of faith that will fill the lonely space in our souls. Perhaps there cannot be a faith of integrity unless first there is a spaciousness in our own natures that invites a Presence. Spaciousness permits a landing pad for revelation's messengers. Do we negate faith to say we may contribute to how we fashion the appearances and behaviors of messengers? I would say not. We lend dignity to the common work of creativity we share with the Great Creator.

The greatest test of my belief that spirituality is a process came about in the aftermath of a serious surgery in my mid-70's. It was first thought I had lymphoma, but after three hours of surgery doctors determined I had a very rare condition requiring excision, lymphangioma. It is a wild growth system of lymph sacs separated from the normal lymph system. In this case the lymph sacs had become a large mass in my abdomen, all of which had to removed because of the original suspicion of cancer. While it was determined I did not have lymphoma, the surgery nevertheless required a resection of the bowel, and included excising two feet of intestine and a small part of the colon. I was hospitalized seven days, and sent home with word it would be a year before I would return to "normal," whatever that was supposed to imply. I could expect six weeks before I could set foot on a tennis court. Meantime, I would wear an abdominal brace four months.

I had approached this surgery with a good deal of equanimity. I am certain the nature of my faith had a good deal to do with my preparedness, as well as the presence of my wife and oldest daughter, and the affection of many good friends who I knew would be praying for my well being and healing. What took me entirely by surprise was the state of my faith and consciousness in the aftermath of surgery.

To put it bluntly, I could not find *any* spiritual faith in my consciousness in the first weeks after surgery. What a shock to find these energies, which had been the core of my life since I was 20 years old, gone. With a body that had been under assault, my psyche in withdrawal, and my insides totally rearranged, I stayed in physical shock, compounded by the dullness from pain medication. But the physical shock was no less than my psychic shock at finding my faith had gone missing.

Truthfully, having read so many glowing testimonies of people undergoing surgery who came through it swimmingly, attributing their rapid brightness and recovery to their faith, I was even more depressed that my experience was turning out to be so entirely opposite. I had lost my faith and was left a psychic zombie. If I had an image of myself at all, as I sat staring for hours, it *was* that of a zombie. Living in appearance, but in reality dead. I felt very dead. Even with the television on, I stared at an edge of the screen, seeing nothing of what was happening at its middle, hearing no discernible sounds that I wanted to pay any attention to. It all seemed to require more effort than I wanted to lend. My capacity to occupy my "observing mind," set apart from whatever I was going through, also left me. I had no observer mind so far as I could tell, which would permit me to observe emotions or thoughts. I was gone somewhere, leaving a zombie behind. This state continued for weeks and then months. My hard-won, vital faith had vaporized in a fire of pain and surgical shock. My heart-filled love for God was gone. My supposedly highly evolved capacity for non-attached observation? Gone.

At some point I awakened enough in my consciousness to feel how desperate I was in my loss, and I turned to an old friend, my Spirit Guide, whom I called "S.G."

"What am I supposed to learn from all this?" I asked him.

Not a word in response. Then, after similar requests in subsequent days, S.G. finally appeared. He said only one word: "Patience." And I did get it. I got it that S.G. was counseling me to believe eventually some meaning would come out of this unexpected loss of faith, would come out of my pain and fear. There would be something here for me if I would not press too hard for an answer.

I think you could say, even when all my conscious faith was obliterated and not available, I truly believed God was there, faith was there, but out of sight at a fundamental place in my being, at bedrock. Also, in a bizarre way, perhaps a stubborn way, I never doubted that my faith and larger consciousness would return. What amazed me was how long a time my faith was absent, and therefore how little I had any personal faith available to participate in the healing process. In this sense, my journey seemed very unlike that of so many other persons of faith, who could draw upon faith's presence and energies almost immediately after their surgeries. I was left to rely upon the healing presence of my wife and daughters, and the prayers and good thoughts of those who cared for and about me in the greatest mortality crisis I had experienced to this point. Nor, should it be forgotten, how much I was assisted in my eventual healing by my nurses and physicians.

I don't know how to account for the kinds of differences in how faith behaves for people. I don't think, of course, that those accounts I read about, where faith was always present in some patients, means they simply had greater faith than I. Explanations will always be faulty in attempting to measure faith, as if it were like measures for flour or sugar. If anything, my experience with loss of faith suggests even more how individualistic one's faith is, and that there are profound variations from person to person.

What I eventually wrote went like this:

"I must be able to accept how profound my faith continued to be, even at a level I was not aware of. I must also be able to accept that how I did my faith journey was simply how I did it, not particularly a model of how other people should, or might, make their own journey of faith when confronted with serious surgery." It became another great lesson in how important it is to learn to accept my own path, my own style and expression of faith, illustrative of how faith may weave its way in and out of my psyche like a hypnotic snake, always there, but sometimes apparent and other times not. My belief in God is like that, too. Always there, the most substantial and filling part of my entire being, but not there, too, scarcely ever in my day to day consciousness, yet the Very Being of my very being. It was as if God one day said to me,

'All right, all right! So you believe in me. Now get on with your life. Live it out, and stop worrying about whether or not you are *thinking* of me often enough. That just wastes your delight and passion in life."

My faith did come back to me, but I had to learn how much my *personal experience* of faith was contingent on having a charged, somewhat intact, body. Which is not to say I did not have a core faith in my soul, even during the worst of times. But at a conscious level, I came to realize pain and suffering can wipe out a personal sense of vital faith. There may be a period of great darkness and dullness one has to go through before a vital faith returns. Faith is embedded in this process of light and darkness, just as spirituality maintains its inherent continuity through our commitment to such a process.

During my darkness, I found my greatest comfort in an incident from Jesus' life, and words attributed to him as he suffered on the cross. At some point he said,

"My God, my God, why have you forsaken me?"

These words, uttered in the throes of extreme pain, strongly suggest Jesus, too, was for a time traversing the utter darkness of a lost God. At his most conscious level, overflowing with suffering, his cry of despair communicates a loss of faith that God was still with him.

I was comforted in knowing Jesus also experienced an entire darkening of his consciousness because of unbearable pain, which caused him to faint. But I was equally comforted by other words Jesus is said to have uttered soon after his protest of despair,

"Father, into Your hands I commend my spirit."

It was as if Jesus were saying, "Despite my suffering, despite my loss of conscious faith, I *have* faith I belong to You, oh God, and that I am your beloved son. Into your hands I commend my spirit."

I have faith even when I do not have faith. This is a remarkable paradox that describes the nature of a faith that rests on *trust* and not *proof.* When S.G. gave me his one-word counsel, "Patience," he was really encouraging me not to leap for an immediate resolution to my faith crisis, but to trust an unfolding process. This process included a long period of darkness and vacuity, when I had no experience of Infinite Being, and no experience of an internally charged faith. But all along I did feel I had some important things to learn from that very rugged experience, an essential part of my journey. I hope I have come out of it a less insistent person, less demanding as to what faith should look like, or be, for me and for others.

I have confidence you will evolve your own way in a spiritual journey. While our questions may appear to be similar, it is likely the answers from "the other side" will be entirely unique to you. Perhaps what each of us must learn is not to push the envelope, to seek, of course, with an open heart, but to allow lots of space and time for answers to our questions to emerge. We must be very, very patient with ourselves. Life, after all, is not easy, nor is human transformation. Our greatest discovery may turn out to be that our faith gifts us with a confidence we belong to God, and our destiny is in the best of all possible hands. We can let go of our worry about what comes next, and matters of exactness.

CHAPTER 6

Waves of Consciousness; Sands of Time

You cannot reconstruct an ocean wave
once it has crashed upon a sandy beach.
You can only turn to waves still forming
far out at sea. No one is without the blessing
of waves, whoever will wade into the blue-
green waters and plant his feet in its bottoms.

These words refer to the futility of attempting to restore forms of energetic expression that are dissolving. They are about a need to let go, to turn where new life is beginning, and to plant our feet as we await its arrival and blessings.

When I first began to write this chapter, I had thought to call some attention to the figure of Jesus for anyone committed to a spiritual journey, regardless of their religious or non-religious background. After all, if giants of history such as Gandhi could cite the influence of Jesus on his wave of non-violent political leadership in India, and a great Muslim Sufi teacher and poet, Rumi, would often include references to Jesus' teachings and life, how could any pilgrim fail to profit from a similar encounter with Jesus?

What I did not expect was how my periodic returns to the Gospels would become significantly different this visit. It sent shock waves rolling through every level of my consciousness, rendering me temporarily stunned, frustratingly inarticulate. More of that later.

I have been especially interested, as my previous chapters indicate, in the theme of authority. I had already theorized, we are increasingly in an age when large numbers of thoughtful and conscious beings have pulled their energies away from reliance on external authority. They have looked increasingly within themselves for wisdom and moral and spiritual guidance. I have identified this shift of consciousness from external to internal as parallel to a shift of religious belief: from a focus of energies on an external authority and deity, to an internal locus of spiritual truth, a consciousness of inner Presence.

What I have come to realize is that for 2,000 years we have been invested in preserving and protecting the continuity of Jesus as God, "Very God of Very God," external and absolute authority. To substantiate this belief, to institutionalize and fixate Jesus consciousness, religious leaders had to create a supporting system of authority known as "apostolic succession," based on the assumption Jesus ordained the Apostle Peter to be his successor. Gradually the dynamic life force Jesus expressed, which questioned the authoritative, fortress structure of Judaic Law and ritualistic practices, became subject itself to attempts to institutionalize it. The construction of a new citadel got underway with a claim an apostolic succession had been created by no less than God (in Jesus), with the authority to speak with God's finality.

Here is how the attempt to box in and control the original power and creativity of the Jesus wave came about: First, the gathering of Christ believers into a citadel, to differentiate those saved for eternity, through the crucifixion of Jesus, from those "lost," or damned, who lived out beyond the fortress moat. Next, construction of the rampart of Apostolic Authority, and after that another rampart: a declaration of selected writings we know as "biblical," were, by the authoritative statement of the Church, infallible and inerrant. Each successive level of authority was constructed to buttress claims to authority by a previous one, and to assert the power and absolute authority of the Church in all things spiritual. In time the Church would assert its claim to authority over all things material and secular as well.

The Church understood itself to be "defender of the faith," existing to insure the finality of Christian beliefs about Jesus and man's eternal destiny. Characteristic of most religious institutions that try to freeze a dynamic process and message, the Christian Church, too, over the centuries abandoned the universality of Jesus' way and message, and surgically joined Jesus' sense of inner authority with an increasingly rigid adulation of Jesus and defensive reliance on its own dominance and power.

It was exactly this kind of slavish reliance on externalized authority that brought Jesus into conflict with provincial and dehumanizing institutions, leaders and religious beliefs and practices, in his own generation. It takes very little reading of the Gospels to recognize Jesus was a real pain to those who insisted the Jewish Law, Jewish commentaries, and Jewish rituals were God's final and complete revelation of God's nature and wishes for human kind, where only strict Jews could be considered God's chosen ones.

We are likely familiar with many accounts of Jesus that underline the clash between his teaching of the universality of God's love and provincial, frozen interpretations of the Law that condemned many segments of humanity. He tells the story of the Good Samaritan to illustrate how the spirit of the law, to help the afflicted, was administered by a "despised" Samaritan traveler on his way from Jericho to Jerusalem, and ignored by "religious types."

Priests bring a woman to him who had committed adultery, who would be stoned until dead under a rigid application of Jewish tribal law, for purposes of trapping the impudent teacher from Nazareth who questioned authority. They asked what he would do with her. As we know, Jesus asked each of them to look into their hearts, and the person who had committed no violation of tribal law could throw the first stone at the woman. As the account goes, no person was so hypocritical as to claim he was "without sin," and they walked away one by one. Jesus turned to the woman and said neither he nor any of the priests had condemned her. She was free to go. (John 8:3-11)

What seems impossible to miss in reading the Gospels is how radically Jesus challenged both the authority of a religious institution and its leadership as a way of breaking open the system so a new consciousness could arise. In doing so he was just as radical in challenging the belief systems and consciousness of those who found their security in externalized and limited authority. Jesus understood very clearly the various systems of authority under which he had grown up, but he also understood with great spiritual vision how continuing, unquestioning dependency on these authorities, ranging from Jewish paternalism to priestly claims, could result in truncated spirits.

While he was certainly not a nihilist, from the records we have, he obeyed an internal authority that urged him to speak, and urged him to live, in ways which broke with tribal consciousness, what we would call orthodoxy. There is no escaping the claim of Gospel accounts that he was, in the potency of his beliefs about the limitations of existing forms of authority, a troublemaker.

Look to words ascribed to Jesus in Matthew: "I have not come to bring peace, but a sword...and a man's foes shall be those of his own household." (Mt. 10:34) It is so ironic how, in our sentimentalized idealization of Jesus, we portray him often in American art as non-Jewish and feminized, almost as if he were gushing love. A more truthful understanding of love might lead us to understand he would likely challenge spiritual dwarfism and egocentric misuses of authority. We need to keep in mind the "Prince of Peace" was a very contentious man, and his courage to contend for a deeper level of consciousness, and a larger vision of God's universal love, may be one characteristic of those who move along in the transformational journey.

The reader may wonder how it is I can bring into question any *assumption* that accounts in the Gospels *must* be treated as "infallible" truth, and yet turn appreciatively to the Gospel record for selected accounts from the life and teachings of Jesus. Well, that is the point. I don't choose an account to prove something to anyone, as if appealing to an absolute external authority. I choose a recorded life event or teaching because it speaks to my inner being. The theologian, Emil Brunner, called this "self-authenticating truth," one that cannot be proved but resonates in our deepest being.

I like to think of my raucous encounters with Jesus as creative struggles. I struggle to hear how and when he speaks to me, and I struggle out of my own heart to determine how some teachings or actions of Jesus are immediately meaningful to me and how others are not. I do not treat what I see and hear as authority, but contend with them as the locus of an original and exceedingly powerful Divine Essence. How could the Gospels sometimes *not* speak to me? My job is to listen, but *not* to listen;

to surrender my consciousness to how this teaching or that teaching may correspond to my nature, my particular spiritual journey, and to the God within me. It is when there is great synchronicity that I feel my consciousness enlarged, I arrive at insight for my journey, and I give praise for revelation.

Obviously, there are very subtle differences here: between surrendering my heart to be open to the Divine Message, and surrendering my soul to the whole body of the Gospels and trying to obey everything I hear and read; between having great respect for the teacher I seek out from time to time, as a guide, and failing to acknowledge my own dignity and capacity for dialogue and speaking out. Contention takes two parties. If Jesus is one, I am the other. The same could be said for any teacher whose essence would appear to suggest Presence to me. I open my heart to their presence and words, but I do not give up my critical faculties, nor do I assume they have any other authority than their authenticity and the transitional role I have given them. It is what comes *through* the teacher that counts, which is why I value Jesus. He, himself, said, it was not him, but the Father through him who spoke and lived. And yet, despite his warnings against believing Jesus could be God, people insisted on making him into one anyway, and to this extent arrested their own furthered consciousness and responsibility.

Do we not treat any teacher to whose energy we are drawn in a similar way? Rumi, the great 13th century Muslim Suffi teacher is a very attractive teacher for me. So much truth seems to come through him of the nature of the Divine, and the nature of the transformational journey. Perhaps this is why Rumi often refers to Jesus. They share a synchronicity of consciousness. It was Rumi's intent, too, to break open the rigidities of Islam with the freshness of Sufi mysticism. He believed inward devotion, ecstatic dance movements and meditation could break open the husk of rigid, intellectualized belief systems, and release the inner vitality of the Divine Presence. He was a great poet in the Persian tradition, and I have been astounded and moved by the leaping unpredictability of his spirit-inspired language. I have friends who don't "get" Rumi at all. The Spirit does not speak to them through Rumi. Which is my point! When we open up our consciousness to the universe, the nature of the faith we hope to nourish and enlighten will hear its *unique and intended* teachers, as surely as mountain streams find the ocean.

Unfortunately, we are much more aware these days of what can happen to any religion that has become a defensive, warring citadel. All those outside are "infidels," or "heretics," or "the damned." The original dynamic of many visions of universal love have been reduced to formulae, authority of priests, sacred books, and visions invested with divine authority. All of them have become separatist and divisive, suspicious and defensive. I said to my wife one day, "Those who maintain their religious beliefs from behind defensive fortress walls of authority, because they fear so many things in this world and in the next, have become so paranoid that if they hear even the rustle of a mouse in the reeds at the edge of the moat, they sound the alarm: 'The enemy is here, the enemy is here!' All the trumpets sound at once, soldiers rush the ramparts with their weapons at ready, looking for the enemy." It is very stressful to a life of faith to feel you must be on guard constantly because there are so many "enemies of the faith."

Clearly, a dynamic understanding of *inner* authority implies a more fluid and flexible understanding of "truth." It is a correspondence of essence between what we see or hear "out there," and what we validate with powerful inner pulsations. This is not the kind of truth many people want or are happy with. They want absolute certainties, blacks and whites. They might say they trust science because what it says can be verified. Except that we are finding out, even in supposedly hard science, tiny grains of new discoveries muck up of the machinery of "scientific certainty." What Einstein once theorized to be true, which invited dismissal from most other scientists, he himself came to reject. And then, surprise! It turned out his theory about the origin of the universe was the "right one" after all. Tomorrow science, so unfortunately deified with as much authority as a god in some quarters, may change its mind again.

In religion, too, we are accustomed to believing truth must be fixed, absolute. We only become angry with the Church when its practices become too hypocritical, or when the gap between a humane life and the demands of the Church become outrageously conflicted. And I speak here of a gap occurring on many occasions over the centuries, up to the present, and not just during the more notable Spanish Inquisition.

It is a difficult step, to feel a fluid competence in your own belly and heart, to identify a capacity within yourself for divining a truth, especially one that others may minimize or demean. If you are true to yourself, it is very likely you will be at odds from time to time with a current set of cultural beliefs and enthusiasms, with the idolization of particular authorities who assure you their view is white in a black and white, polarized world.

This past week I found certain accounts of Jesus' life, and other of his teaching, speaking to me. Making trouble for me, lots of trouble. I had to contend with Jesus, wrestle. I usually do. I don't propose leaving this man trapped inside a black leather book until Sunday, or Easter, or Christmas, when we all break out singing. Jesus is not simply "history." I believe Jesus' life was, and is, so powerful, that God will continue to speak through his life and ministry.

I want to position myself to hear, to identify what is true for me for this week, even commanding. I do this not to obey a demand that I grind out the same dead or dying creeds or statements of belief I held 50 years ago. I do it out of a ground of confidence in my oneness with God, and a belief I can find what God's intention is for me to speak, write, and live. I will neither reject all biblical accounts out of hand as irrelevant, nor will I surrender my critical capacity to recognize truth when I see it.

The journey of transformation does not consist of seeing how faithful we can be to Jesus, it is seeing how faithful we can be to his *calling*, that all beings understand themselves to be loved by God and to be one with God. Transformation, as a process, is living out as faithfully as possible the compulsions of truth and love within us. It is not carefully plotting each "religious" step we will take in order to "be transformed," which sounds dreadfully similar to "Steps" we must take to "be saved." Transformation is carried forward in the caravan of obedience and responsiveness to the deepest within us. It is a path we understand to be uniquely ours, though all souls are on this journey, conscious of it or not. The journey is subject to dangerous, surprising turns, and remarkable illuminations of the soul. If you would hang onto anything, buckle up to the heart.

If there is an intention for this book, it is to describe the dynamic character of transformation, based upon belief in our oneness with God. Certainly, I am encouraging the reader to see how easily we fall into a trap of hanging the authority for our lives on someone else's coat hook, someone else's journey. Keep in mind, it is God in YOU, creating your own courageous journey, not Jesus' journey, not mine, not Rumi's. I have spoken of some of my own authority and belief traps along the way, and some of my illuminations. I hope the examples may encourage your own journey. But at last, whatever traps you fall into, they will be yours, not anyone else's to contend with, just as your discoveries will feel excitingly and personally redemptive.

Let me share another recent story from my journey. As I was arriving at the realization that in my deepest soul recesses I had still kept Jesus on the cross, had maintained him as my final authority at some obscure level, I knew in my heart what I was being asked to do: let go of this Jesus, give him up. I felt I had to be firm, insistent with myself: *give Jesus up!*

My mind drifted back to the words I had written weeks before, recorded on the opening page of this chapter: a wave had completed itself, and was losing its previous form into the sands. Connections with the demand I was hearing to give Jesus up. My mind drifted to another experience, tears of unknown origin appearing at the corner of my eyes, rolling down my cheeks...a grief unaccounted for. Another connection. I was grieving a loss even before I consciously became aware of what the loss was: Jesus. If I had been more passive, hung on more, not faced the reality of "My Jesus" death already in my inner being, I would not have been able to make *this* death of an idealized and authoritative Jesus final. I might, desperately, have attempted to keep Jesus from dying. I would not have been free to welcome the next incoming, refreshing wave of consciousness and authority, God within me. My energy would have been split between a dying form of consciousness and one initiating its birth.

In the shift of consciousness I have described, I had flashes of being a Judas Iscariot, betraying Jesus, giving him over to death. And, in fact, that was precisely what was occurring at an internal level. I was Judas, part of the mob, giving over the body of my revered, beloved, externalized Jesus to the cross.

I suspect many persons, who have been locked into a system of beliefs that gave them great security and love, have felt terribly guilty for giving up the *form* of their belief structure. Have you ever thought of yourself as a Judas? In order to become truly free, to welcome a fresh wave of consciousness, any of us may have to become Judas, willing to betray the familiar associations and beloved objects of our existing be- liefs. We must become Abraham, prepared to slay his beloved son, Isaac, because it is the angelic command of truth.

While I had expected to find writing about Jesus the most fluid of all my chapters, it turned out by far to be the most demanding and difficult. The reasons, as I complete my 8th draft, and at least 30 hours of effort, have painfully and slowly emerged. To encounter the most unconscious and entrenched fixations related to my bonding with Jesus, I had to gain some separation from him. And then I had to kill him, be willing to feel as guilty as a Judas Iscariot. It was a required stay in the wilderness. I slept poorly. I wrote passionately and compulsively, trying to hurry along whatever was happening, all to no avail. The next morning I would read my words and realize the chapter was not complete. It was tortured in syntax, full of errors, peppered with boring repetition. How could that be, when the night before, exhausted, I was saying to myself: "Finally, it is done!" In the light of morning hours, I would continue to find I was still hanging on, still lying to myself and my reader in some way I could not identify. Authenticity still eluded me.

My wife interceded momentarily in my wilderness experience. She has had her own wilderness experiences. She understands wilder- ness is part of the journey, essential to a continuing transformation of consciousness. We both believe spiritual consciousness requires many deaths, and that without deaths a new consciousness cannot be born. She also understands much of our wilderness journey must be done alone. But when she offered to do some eye movement desensitization work

(EMDR) with me, to facilitate the process I was going through, I immediately understood she could be my guide. Not one who stays in my wilderness, but one who enters it to assist.

I had expected what I would discover in her work with me would be dark and lonely, perhaps even edging the Satanic. I expected my consciousness to become rough terrain, to be jerked around by alternating, driven energies and a need to collapse. I expected to hover at the cliff edges of perfectionism and total disillusionment. I envisioned alternating between despair I would never get the chapter on Jesus "right," and what seemed like an unjustified confidence God was still with me in speaking what I had to. As is so often the case, what I expected and what actually occurred in Linda's work with me, were surprisingly different.

Both Linda and I had profited from doing EMDR work. As a clinical psychologist, she had specialized in its use in treating severe trauma before her retirement. I had great confidence, based on past experience, that this method could help me access the spiritual trauma of my wilderness. As it turned out, my confidence was valid. But to my great surprise, the wilderness that appeared to me in a resting period after eye movements was not desert. It was a secluded, peaceful spot in the mountains. The terrain itself was, indeed, rough, but I seemed to be sitting on a large rock, quite at peace. There were fresh springs to the back of where I sat, and a small, cold stream of water flowing down the hill beside me. On both sides, nestled into the rocks, was beautiful, soft moss. And as my eyes moved about, I could see a great variety of small, colorful and bright, flowers. The rock on which I sat?

As I re-write this paragraph for the 9th time, I see with the eyes of faith what the rock *means*, its dynamic character. I see how firm and reliable it is. I see it supports my evolving conscious. I see I have created it through years of a risk-taking faith. I see it is a gift of revelation. It is the Presence of Being Itself.

My wilderness experience was one of beauty and hope at its deepest level, no matter what kind of death I was going through at a more conscious level. I knew that eventually my psyche would be unified, and I would feel as bright and at peace as my surroundings in the wilderness scene.

It is all so human to want to hang onto the familiar, the wave that has already blessed us. But it is also futile and painful to try and collect those waters from the sands once they have performed the task for which they were intended. We will never know the blessings still forming, unless we are willing to turn our eyes, limbs and bodies toward them, and open our hearts and arms.

CHAPTER 7

What a New Consciousness Looks Like

In the previous chapter I suggested faith consciousness is awakening to awareness of the Essence of Being within one's self. This consciousness is accompanied by a simultaneous shift of attention from externalized authority to internal authority.

Absolute Authority vested in the Church, Scripture, religious leaders, Jesus himself, or the State, may be respected with appreciation and gratitude for whatever goodness and grace these systems have brought to us. But each must also be subjected to the careful scrutiny of the heart, to see which beliefs and practices have embraced and uplifted human welfare and consciousness, and which have created guilt, shame, and hostile estrangement toward "unbelievers."

I have also suggested there is much to be gained in our own transformation of consciousness, by positioning ourselves for engagement with Jesus. He is likely to continue to challenge us, whether or not we have a Christian background, perhaps each time from a different place in the Gospel accounts. The same may be said for other historically power-ful spiritual teachers, that we may be challenged by their essence if we become familiar with their teachings. We may find their truth resonates within us.

I wonder if I might turn to experiences in my own historical tradi-tion, and to an enigmatic teaching attributed to Jesus, to illustrate how we may participate in the same spiritual consciousness, though we exhib-it many surface differences of belief and practice? I am going to propose to you that the *new* (new to some of us, familiar to others) *consciousness is that we are one with Being and one with each other.* New consciousness *is* the church of our day. It is the church without walls. It is characterized by a consciousness unhindered by space and time.

I had a very vivid and powerful dream 40 years ago. At the time I was director of a college undergraduate counseling center, as well as being an adjunct professor in a graduate master's degree counseling program. These were jobs I enjoyed and that were challenging. Nevertheless, from time to time I wondered if I was carrying out my "calling," having been an ordained minister for 18 years.

In my dream several persons who comprise a pastoral committee are taking me in a car to see the church where I will eventually be minister. We go up into beautiful hills, where the well-maintained road twists back and forth, and eventually I see a lovely, white clapboard church on a hill-side, nestled among the trees. I am very excited at the prospect of being a pastor at this beautiful church, though there seem to be no houses in the vicinity and I am struck by its isolation.

I expect the driver of the car to turn off at the next intersection on a road that will take us closer to the white clapboard church. Instead he keeps going, turns downhill instead of uphill. We take similar switch-backs to wind down the mountain. Soon we have lost track of the pretty church altogether, but I expect we will come to another soon. I hope it will be just as attractive. Instead the road we are on becomes more traveled, with more cars, and there are houses all about. I see we are coming into a village, and we drive into the very center of it. I see there is a huge fair going on, large numbers of people at tables, eating and visiting, games, energetic activities. The driver stops and I realize we are at our destination. The dream ends.

When I first had the dream it made a dramatic impression on me because it helped me redefine my "calling." I was not to be the pastor of a beautiful little church isolated from homes and commerce. I was to be among the people, where the real energy was.

Only in the past few weeks have I come to understand the dream was not just about the nature of my life's task. It was about who and what constituted "The Church."

I believe the locus of Divine energy for our day is not a church with four walls and a ceiling, however beautiful the setting may be. The locus of Divine energy is wherever we are. It is in the village, in the excitement of our human interaction. It may *even* be in an attractive church building if *you* are there! But one must no longer assume we only meet God in the church, or synagogue or mosque.

Jesus once said, "Wherever two or three are gathered together in my name, there am I also." Just what does it mean, "My name?" Well, we know what we have been told, that it means those who meet as confessed believers in Jesus as Lord and Savior; so, if only two or three believers are together, Jesus is there, too.

But suppose "My name" refers to the *essence* of Jesus? His integrity, his compassion, his courage, his fidelity to what he believed to be the voice of God? Is it not more likely, given Jesus' express teaching of the universality of God's love, that the essence of Jesus is present in *any* gathering of two, three, or more, where the energies of those persons are set on truth, integrity, or intentions and expressions of compassion?

I think Jesus was far more radical than we can possibly imagine, inasmuch as the essence which he himself drew upon was so humanely ethical, and so liberated from divisiveness and prejudice. He was radical enough, in my estimation, to have included in his "two or three," any beings whose consciousness was organized around authenticity, integrity and compassion, be they Christian, Buddhist, Taoist, Hindi, or Muslim. And yes, I believe agnostic or atheist.

I must admit to a long-time aversion to the descriptive phrase "God-consciousness." I suspect I thought it sounded too airy, spacey, and lacked the masculinity and grounding in reality I required of my religion. "Jesus-consciousness" seemed no improvement. My wife, Linda, went further to observe that the term, "God," itself is so encrusted with hoary stories, dogma, and human contaminations that she prefers "Spirit." Spirit has a more fluid, dynamic connotation, not subject to time, space or human entrapment.

A commonality of language does help us communicate, but I think we will have to give up on our passion for exactness when it comes to defining the ineffable. The best I will be able to do is to find a linguistic home for the polarities within myself, an anthropomorphic disposition that wants to make God human, and a mystical respect that experiences oneness with The One as a fluid, energetic charge. I encourage my reader to find his or her own best language to express the transformational consciousness I have been describing, this sea of Being where our language is at best a frail raft.

What does the community of this new consciousness look like, aside from not being contained in a mosque, church, or synagogue, and not being defined by its creeds or an external authority which governs it?

Obviously, those of the new community are obedient, but to their inner voice   rather than to any church leader, collective leadership, book, or set of writings. To the extent they hear the same, or a similar, command for ethical action, they "become" an expression of the larger church of consciousness. It is how energy gathers itself for the tasks of truth, resistance to wrong, and compassion. It defines the subtle meaning of "two or three in my name."

In our generation, because of the internet, and widespread information availability and communication, we are likely to see thousands of gatherings that share a similar consciousness. Though separated by thousands of miles, by oceans and mountains, these "church members," as I have defined the new church, often share a deep, ethical, and humane vision. Here are people from Germany, Norway, Morocco, Kenya, and the United States. What are they doing? They share a participating faith characterized by similarity of thought, energy and passion, and a conviction the environment must be protected. Or they share a faith that a new holocaust is underway in the Sudan, and that we must intervene to save millions of human beings. This is the new church, as I create the meaning of Jesus' words to construct my faith. It includes people from every nation, and from every conceivable range of belief, religious and humanist.

Undoubtedly, the notion of a "church of consciousness," one defined by its focus on integrity or compassion, not its doctrinal beliefs, may arouse disagreement and even animosity from those who insist the Spirit can only be found within a structure made of stones, whether those stones are a church building or a set of beliefs said to constitute orthodoxy. For persons who believe only Muslims will enter paradise, or those who believe only Christians who confess Jesus as Savior will be "saved" for eternity, walls that separate are a necessity. Without the walls, how are you going to keep the sheep and the goats apart? A rigidly defined faith is essential to the security of those who need it and essential to the survival of the institutions invested in claims to absolute, divinely ordained authority. It is transformational consciousness that has the dynamic capacity for bridging differences, and contains the collective energy needed to help people recognize they are one. And one with the One.

There is another point I would like to make about God-Consciousness and its capacity for universal oneness. Within such consciousness there is no need to try and convert anyone to a single set of beliefs in order to "save" them, or reassure ourselves of the validity of our faith. We have quite enough to do to take care of our own consciousness, our fidelity to the best within us, to observing our authenticity or lack of it. To be a fully conscious being is a truly demanding path. There isn't much time or space for agendas, hidden or otherwise.

Oddly, one of the more difficult aspects of the new consciousness is in learning how to be more patient and compassionate with ourselves. If we are committed to truth, justice and compassion, we will find our brothers and sisters who share our faith, and they will be called by many names and come from many nations and faiths. We may need all the help we can get from their wisdom and consciousness to encourage our journey of transformation. I find it interesting that so many of our closest friends believe themselves to be agnostics. We share a certain kind of energy with these particular beings. We're drawn to their humanistic convictions, their desire to affect public decisions in favor of those who lack power, and yes, their sense of humor. They constitute members of my wife's and my "church," a church without walls.

Is God-consciousness superior to tribal consciousness? To Muslim consciousness? To Jesus consciousness? It's the wrong question, once again the subtle trap of creating divisions. Who is right, who is wrong? Who is superior to the other?

The only way to avoid this comparison trap is to have enough identification with universal consciousness so that you don't fall into it. To be one with Being is to see our oneness with all beings. It is to see all the barriers falling down, or never there in reality, between us and other beings.

To see with the Eternal Eye may be to look upon many dimensions of learning, and human beings living out simultaneous states of consciousness alongside one another. Our task is to maintain with fidelity the gift of consciousness *we* have been given, and with which we have been blessed. If this involves a challenge to other dimensions of consciousness unlike ours, so be it, but let none of us make the assumption we occupy a "superior place," no matter what our beliefs. It is just such an assumption that divides us, one from the other, and drapes us with a protective arrogance that muffles our hearts.

We read fairly often these days of how some "liberal" denominations are losing membership. Sometimes the "liberal" faith itself is blamed, with fundamentalist critics smugly pointing to the mega-church successes of conservative churches. At other times pastors themselves are put to blame, for one reason or another. I think it is most important that pastors not be blamed for a drooping membership list. I would suggest looking, instead, to where the energy is moving. I think it has left the church with four walls and that many persons of liberal consciousness have followed the energy, even if they don't know it. I doubt if you will find many liberals who have left their churches whose behavior has changed all that much. If anything, they may be more active in supporting charitable programs and writing letters to magazines and newspaper editors that underline their ethical convictions. What they are doing less of is expending energy in support of the institutional church, and being dependent on external voices of authority.

Even those who have left the church with some guilt, and feel something is therefore "missing," realize they have left because something they sought was not there. I suggest that what they seek is consciousness of the One within. They will "find" as they are found.

Rather than rail against those who have "left the church," it behooves those who remain to recognize that an old, 2000 year old, form is likely dying, the mega-church and its hyper rock-groups and reliance on charisma notwithstanding. If there is a place for an institutional church today, it seems to me it will be in recovering the excitement of pastors looking out on congregations of persons who are taking responsibility for the creation of their own vital faith. Think what it would mean for members to share their visions, and for the church to be able to draw from, say, 200 or 300 imaginative creations of what faith has become for individual parishioners, and to celebrate that rather than worrying about what's "normative." In this sense, a religious leader is an encourager of visions, teaching a congregation faith visions are particular to the individual, possibly inspiring to others, but not normative for faith. A pastor is no longer an authority figure, but an enabler for personal faith, for responsible consciousness, a stimulus to individual faith-creativity, a respected person familiar with a tradition who is committed to their own journey of creating a vital faith.

CHAPTER 8

Spiritual Agnosticism

I picked up the "Week in Review" section of the *New York Times* and began reading a lead article about the children of Africa. Halfway through I was in minor shock, feeling nauseated. I literally could not continue reading. The gist of the article: several million children of Africa are dying of starvation, disease and violence. Other perhaps millions are in poverty, serfdom, and without at least one parent because of war and AIDS.

I wondered if it was just me, a sudden assault of exceptional sensitivity to pain, so I asked my wife if she had read the article.

"Oh, my God! I started to and couldn't go on it made me so ill," she responded.

"Me, too," I said.

Did it help to share the horror? Perhaps *ours*, some. But *the* horror, the suffering of millions of children, is still there. There is no immediate resolution in sight because of the conditions that spawned their poverty, disease and starvation in the first place.

Shortly afterward, when I was preparing to re-write a chapter in this book, I continued to be haunted by the pictures accompanying the *Times* article. In my mind I found myself crying out loudly, "Goddamn you! Goddamn you! Where *are* you?" The irony did not escape me later that I was crying out for God to damn God for the widespread suffering inflicted on innocents.

Is *this* God at whom I am provoked to rage the same Inner Presence of peace I have written of previously, the God of my very being, the God of Infinite Wisdom? Is this the same One who has created all that is? The very same. I may have been more profane than the words I have recorded. The God who has won my love and fidelity is the creator of a world that includes at its core death and immense suffering. And I hate it. At times I am broken by it. Unlike many brave and compassionate souls who move into the core of suffering in order to offer compassion and healing, I often turn away from suffering because my system can't tolerate it. At times I weep because of it.

How is it possible to reconcile an awesome and grateful sense of God with the nature and extent of human suffering in our world? It is the very, very old issue, from biblical Job to the Greek Stoic philosopher, Epictetus, whenever humans have asked the great questions about life, up to the present. If God is all-powerful and all loving, yet does not resolve the problem of profound human suffering, either he is *not* all-powerful or he is not all loving. I think that was how Epictetus put it in support of atheism.

I won't attempt to address all the arguments or reasons good thinkers, good men and women, have put forth in attempting to resolve the dilemma of faith versus repulsion, or faith versus doubt. Partly this is due to my own bias that a satisfactory resolution of the dilemma through reasoning is neither convincing nor possible.

The harder demand laid upon us by existence, I believe, is evolving a capacity for containment. By containment I mean letting go of the pressure we feel to "solve" the dilemma of faith and doubt. By containment I mean giving up the idea we have to be one "place" or the other, either a believer or an agnostic. Suppose we have a consciousness that is capable of observing faith and doubt within ourselves. Suppose we have a capacity to honor and experience each *deeply*, without making a demand on ourselves we get rid of one or the other? Sometimes we feel almost ashamed that we can think opposites and feel opposites, as if we are being bad little thinkers—or agnostics—or believers. I think it is our heart that is capable of tolerating opposites. Our heart, with a much larger sense of humor and unpredictability than the rest of us, seems to delight in paradox. Our heart and its companions: intuition, creativity and imagination.

Suppose, then, that we don't *have* to label ourselves *agnostic* because we have pieces of a strong agnostic consciousness? Suppose we don't *have* to label ourselves *believers* because we have in our consciousness pieces that can experience awe and cosmic imagination.

Are there not some advantages to a faith that is flexible enough to be open to our doubts and rage over injustice and human suffering, our anger with a deity who "apparently" does nothing? For one thing, if you are a person of faith, rage with God may be honest. You don't settle for a glib rationalization. You face squarely how difficult it may be at times to sustain faith in the face of immense ignorance and human suffering. For another thing, your experience of human indignation, rage and grief is likely to bring your heart closer to non-believers who are at work trying to heal pain because human beings are "all we've got." Your own skepticism will open your heart to your brother agnostic humanitarians.

My agnosticism does have another side to it. It is the side that may bring into question the "convenient skepticism" of agnostics that relies on the limitations of logic and time-bound rationalism. In contrast with many persons of faith, I believe if I limited my consciousness about the possible existence of God to reasoning, I would call myself an agnostic, too. The exclusive path of reasoning is a box. If you take that path you become obliged to reach conclusions I think are consciousness-limiting. I find it useful to be agnostic about the exclusive employment of reasoning to arrive at metaphysical conclusions. I am also agnostic about the assumption time-bound conclusions constitute ultimate reality. I believe ultimate reality is neither time-bound nor space-bound. I believe, therefore, that it is useful to be agnostic about the conclusion atheists sometimes reach, that there cannot be a god who would either create a world in which there is so much suffering, or who would fail to intervene in it. My agnosticism says all the answers are not in yet, and that some of the most important ones lie beyond space and time.

Some of you familiar with the Old Testament will recall reading of David's anger with God. Apparently the Jewish faith was able to tolerate and even honor anger toward God as a deeply human response to life events. My belief is that authentic, deeply experienced rage and grief *are* sacred events. When I practiced psychotherapy, I was moved to awe over and over again as my clients reached into their souls and experienced incredible pain of sorrow or rage. These deeply felt and expressed human feelings carried the energy of the Divine. I will never be able to convince anybody of that, I know, but some of my readers will understand it because they have experienced such awe. I have no wish to exclude human anguish from anyone's faith life. I believe what is deeply humane is invested with sacred energy. I believe the authentic, deeply humane, is Being incarnate.

Permit me to return to my fairly stubborn defense of agnosticism as a human quality in each of us that needs to be owned and integrated with our faith, rather than being shown the door. Frankly, I don't want to give up *any* part of my consciousness entirely. Like all the rest of me, it is my inheritance. It is a gift of creation. It is an achievement of my experience and imagination. I will investigate it, experience it, however scary and at odds with other parts of me it may be at times. And I will especially try to experience and acknowledge my agnosticism when most of the rest of me is psychically shutting down.

I not only want agnosticism in the same house as the rest of my nature, I want to call upon it to give my faith a kind of muscularity. When I am too attached to my ideals, too much in flight, and not aware of it, I want my agnosticism to ground me. I want it to bring me down to the earth by questioning my thought forms and assumptions, my emotions, my relationships, my ideas. Agnosticism is my ballast, my warning my soul is becoming ethereal before its time. I suppose that is why I treasure my friendship with those whose agnosticism has been hard won. These are people who have asked the serious questions of life about our universe, nature, and human confusion and suffering. This is not to say *all* agnostics are of the kind I describe: thoughtful, open, intelligent and truly reflective. Some are more dogmatic, more closed, and have more fixed ideas than some fundamentalists I have known. I don't like to spend time with these folks. A true exchange of ideas, authenticity and emotions is impossible.

In my cloistered, sadistic self I sometimes wish I could bring an arrogant agnostic together with an overbearing religious type and let them go at it. Like pit bulls. I can tell you, both would emerge wounded but unscathed in their beliefs. The distance between them is enormous and paper-thin simultaneously. The extremes of fundamentalism and the atheism are failures of imagination.

We are often oriented toward solution and control. We see a problem and we want to solve it. We see an aberration and we want to correct it. In this sense it is understandable why people would be impatient with a path that presses forward less, one that relaxes and goes within, and seeks containment of apparent opposites. And by containment I don't mean control, which implies force and pressure, trying to "make" doubt go away, or getting rid of faith as soon as possible, because in the face of so much suffering, to have a faith simply <u>must</u> be absurd.

If containment is not putting pressure on, then what is it? It is a process of moving inward to the heart, so the mind, which *always* presses for a solution in order to reduce anxiety, begins to quiet. The body begins to quiet. One starts to observe from a center of peacefulness, comes to observe without judgment faith-thoughts *and* doubt- thoughts, faith *and* doubt emotions, faith *and* doubt cellular charges. This inner nature perceives consciousness to be a continuing process that engages each, and values each. From this deep place in our psyche we trust that every aspect of consciousness, such as faith *and* doubt, will reach compatibility in a unified life, thought and ethic. Please note that resolution is not forced by anxiety or idealism. Resolution occurs as normal process in the evolution of consciousness.

It is not always pleasant to be at home with one's agnosticism. For example, say your friends or family members have found a charismatic religious hero or teacher. You have studied with this teacher, too. You have tried to stay open, but all kinds of warning bells go off inside you. Doubts as to the authenticity of the teacher appear. But when you express your reservations you are accused of sour grapes. Your reservations are dismissed with sarcasm by the teacher. You are shunned by other students.

Or suppose everyone is laughing at a joke that has derisive ethnic overtones. Your questioning the intent and effect of this joke sets off alarms and blocks laughter. Your skepticism about the appropriateness of the joke may prompt you to say the joke was not funny, and in poor taste. I don't see how it is possible to have a truly strong, ethical and individualistic faith without the support of a skeptical competence. I *need* my agnosticism to bring into question what *should* to be brought into question, so I am not impaled on the spear of my naivety or need to be agreeable.

As for the larger issues of creation and human suffering, I don't want to have to be in denial as to how our earthly life sometimes stinks. Or as the bumper sticker has it, "Life sucks, and then you die." I don't want to be the mother who refuses to notice her daughter's behavior is self-destructive, who refuses to heed her doubts about her husband's behavior with their daughter. Human life was, at one time, brief, painful and mean. Life now is *long*, painful and *still* all too mean. It would be strange for a life of authentic faith if we were not sometimes angry with God for not doing it all better.

My aunt on my mother's side lived a very painful life. Her mother died of tuberculosis when she was only 9, and her father in all likelihood sexually molested her after that. Her older sister also died of tuberculosis shortly after marrying and giving birth to a child. Aunt Emerald was unable to form emotional attachments with men or women, She had a psychotic break, I had to commit her, and she was diagnosed as mentally ill. Within the enlightened California mental health system, my aunt was fairly comfortably hospitalized for over 40 years. Over that period of time, I came to know her as well as anyone likely could have.

One day when I was visiting Aunt Emerald, and had taken her out to lunch, she said she had always remembered a little verse that had been told to her by a man she knew when she was quite young. I asked her what the verse was.

She sniffed a couple of times, looked at me as if deciding whether or not she wanted to repeat it, then said:

"When all is said and done, life at its best is none too good."

I was very moved at her recitation. My aunt never said much during our visits. She just enjoyed her little glass of wine and smacked her lips over her lunch or dinner. But what little she said that day had an arresting honesty and irony about it. I would not have wanted her to pretend to a faith that would have been inconsistent with her nature and her experience.

I believe we must treasure, or at the very least value, our capacity for asking questions of our world and our faith. How shall a personal faith become dynamic without the question-maker in us? A healthy, integrated agnosticism saves us from being stunted, from staying in the second grade of our faith, when we need to move on in the school for consciousness.

I don't know when it was humans first began to realize that if their automobiles were to go faster, and still get the same gas mileage, something in the shape of their cars would have to be streamlined. The same evolution has occurred with air flight, discovering how to make flying smoother, and airplanes and rockets more aerodynamic.

Whatever metaphor we may use, it all comes out to the same place: if our souls are to move at an increasing vibratory frequency, we must get rid of the fixed designs of our faith and thinking that hold us back. We must be open to the development of visionary fuels that fire us, to the construction of faith vehicles that are substantial enough to sustain us as we explore inner and outer space.

A thought came to me a few days ago: the purpose of life is refinement of choices. I actually am not even sure what that means, but I felt at the time there was a truth to it. I do believe there are probably many ways we learn to refine our choices, if that means making our choices wiser, kinder and more courageous. We will, perhaps, make fewer choices but more telling ones. Is the refinement of choices a re-working of our consciousness, in much the same way a cook makes a loaf of bread from scratch? She gathers the dough, kneads it, rolls it, pounds it, squeezes it, stretches it, adds flour, pushes at it, kneads it, adds liquid, squeezes it, rolls it out, forms it to fit the loaf pan.

CHAPTER 9

Toward an Understanding of Mysticism

There is a common belief mysticism is a method of prayer or meditation that achieves direct access to God without the need for the mediation of shamans, Church, rituals, scriptures or priests. One imagines a god who occupies the penthouse, and mysticism as an express elevator that bypasses all intervening floors.

The elevator metaphor exposes why words are important in framing thought. For example, "direct access to God" suggests a spatial way of thinking about the nature of God: God is distant—transcendent—vastly separated from our inconsequential lives and infinitesimal consciousness. If God is indescribably distant, then mysticism has to be an extraordinarily equipped spiritual practice to transport us, and the mystic unusually trained and exotically fueled.

All of this is nonsense, of course, and the metaphor is entirely misleading once we accept, or believe, God is inherent in creation, and that His Being permeates all of life. It is not unusual spiritual equipment or exotic spiritual fueling that "gets" us to God. It is an act of our own consciousness that allows us to experience the presence of Being, unbound by time or space. That act of consciousness is called faith. Faith as I understand it is a commitment to heart energies that transform thinking. The great mathematician and philosopher, Pascal, concluded reason would take him only so far, and that eventually he had to "take the leap of faith." We have to commit to an inner repository of ourselves that is not-thinking, non-reasoning, if we want a faith daring and potent enough to upgrade our consciousness.

If we start with an assumption of the "presentness" of God, then the question becomes, how do we position our hearts and minds so we *experience* our union with the One? Or, to put it another way, how do we learn to merge our *particular* consciousness with the unbounded, universal consciousness that permeates all of life? In one way, the answer to this question is quite simple: turn an intentionally blank, uncluttered mind toward our hearts while we maintain steady breathing, and we are there. We are at a place in our own being—non-mind and open—where we may experience what I think of as a universal dimension of ourselves. Being Itself.

If a reader should say I am arbitrarily naming an experience as "oneness with Being," I would do more than agree with them. I would say I am creating a faith that *defines* the experience. A small bit of awe can arise within us from any number of experiences: viewing majestic mountains we have never seen before, a moment of quiet heart energies passing between us and another, our recognition of great courage in a friend during her illness, an unusual feeling of sublime peacefulness during a meditation. You will have your own list of awe-inspiring experiences. There is no *reason* one <u>must</u> associate a god with any of these experiences. On the other hand, there is no reason *not to* experience a sense of Being. One could say some have organized their "faith" to deny any association of awe-inspiring events with a god, and others of us have created a faith that links the experience of awe with Being. I define my view of metaphysical reality through the prism of a faith I have created. One might say that my faith makes possible the echo effect of the Presence of Being, and the magnification of awe, when I have experienced something awe-inspiring. My awe often carries within it an edge of *sacredness.*

I think we all create bins and explanations for our experiences. A person who excludes God from her mind and imagination will find some other way to describe her experience of non-thinking, and the effects of concentrating her attention on her heart. Her faith may be suspicious of words, like "awe," "sacred," and "Being." But everyone has a faith, if by that we mean what we believe about the universe, the world we inhabit, and our own natures. Our differences are in how we inhabit our faith, or populate it, arrange it, or decorate it. In my opinion, our differences are often defined by the imaginative vitality we give to our faith. For some, the idea that humans might rely on "heart energies" for their own shifts of consciousness and the healing of human suffering is unscientific at best, and an absurd and dangerous superstition at worst. For others of us, we can't imagine a fully satisfying life without the imaginative heart mythology we can neither prove nor need to prove, but believe.

Someday science may be able to identify a non-matter heart beneath, or in the proximate vicinity of, our organic hearts. For more than 40 years we have been able to take photographs of non-matter energy forms that are both in and surrounding the body. These energy forms, often called "auras," are not visible to most persons under ordinary conditions. A small percentage of our population, often called "sensitives," sees auras readily and naturally. The time may be around the corner when our scientific methodology will become so precise we will be able to <u>map</u> the energies that form an invisible substratum <u>beneath</u> every aspect of our physical bodies. But for now, persons of faith must rely on their inner experience, their capacity for imaginative creativity, and only very occasional experiences of literally seeing the energy fields I have described.

We would do well to keep in mind that Traditional Chinese Medicine brings to the table of physical healing and faith a venerable history of energy consciousness. The mapping of energy meridians lies behind their concept that the task of the physician is to keep the system in balance, and the belief that disease is an imbalance of the human energy system. Acupuncture and acupressure courses are now embedded in some medical schools, and their practice is so widespread that it is probable most of the readers of this book have gone to practitioners for treatments. The entire background of this practice rests on intuited perception, mapping of energy fields derived from self-authentication, and observation of successful healing. Yet, meridians and a set of beliefs that resulted in their mapping, would be difficult to prove within the limitations of our thinking and our technology.

There are always further questions that evolve from a mystical practice, aside from its validity. How do we learn to listen for the *intention* of Being for our lives? What is being asked of us? What is being asked of us socially and ethically? What does God want *for* us? We may be ready to use our faith and intuition to ask what God wants *from* us because guilt and responsibility are familiar companions. It may be more difficult to understand there are a large range of gifts the Divine wants to give to us, that He wants *for* us, such as our personal empowerment and compassion for ourselves, an increased capacity for delight. If there is any one thing I have experienced over and over again in the life of faith, it is that of surprise. Surprise at what I am being asked to do. Surprise at the unexpected gifts I have been given. Surprise that almost everything I have thought about a life of faith has undergone ceaseless reconstruction. It is a reconstruction of faith that was absolutely required of me, and I assume always will be required, if God is the Creator of new forms of life.

If you should call yourself a mystic, bear in mind it doesn't mean anything special. It is just a way to understand your spiritual path better. But you don't have to live in a cave, be filled with a steady stream of visions, or become a vegetarian. Mainly, you spend time looking into your heart, observing how your mind behaves, and by silence and reflection you learn to become more conscious of Presence. After awhile you find yourself doing what most decent mystics do: they simply go about their business in the steady confidence the Divine is with them. You probably won't actually *think about* God very much, if at all. The Divine is the *assumption of your Being*, so you just do what you need to do, and what you are drawn to do. You go home, have a good dinner, play, and have a good night's sleep. Above all you have no need to *talk about* God, as if He/She were an object. That externalizes Being, which is something of an embarrassment. The psychological effect of realizing the Divine has become an assumption of your being is often experienced as balance, or integration. There is less division in one's consciousness between Spirit and matter, or Sacred and profane, as if in reality there *were* no difference.

It could be said, if there is such a thing as an ultimate faith consciousness, it is when there is no distinction between the sacred and the commonplace. Seamless perceptions and experiences become more familiar for the person on a spiritual journey. We find ourselves carrying our delight in Being into welcoming a wide range of human experiences and creativity that at one time we might have rejected or ignored.

Over-romanticized as it might sound, there is a truth to the mystic's perception of all of life as a celebration. Transformation is a quite odd process in a way, a funny thing: it changes us the way *we need* to be changed, not the way we might idealize, or the way *someone else* is changed.

I don't quibble much with the several definitions of mysticism I find in more recent and better dictionaries. They seem quite close to what I have already described. However, there is one I am especially fond of, perhaps because it validates the role intuition plays in my spiritual journey. According to this definition, mysticism is:

"The doctrine that asserts the possibility of attaining an
intuitive knowledge of spiritual truths through meditation."
Webster's New World Dictionary

Webster's definition of mysticism contends we can know important truths directly through intuition, as over and against a process of reasoning and logic. The definition also suggests there are practices such as meditation that predispose us toward spiritual consciousness. The Webster is limited, of course, in not being able to describe intuition more broadly. We know that many streams of thought, emotion, ethical considerations, and experience are flowing *into* the sea of intuition regularly, unless we have constructed dams to keep them out of our imaginative faith. Intuition is organically changed and renewed on a constant basis by so many aspects of our experience and consciousness.

It is probably true that some persons are, by genetic and environmental disposition, more intuitive than others. They have usually discovered early on in life that what they intuit is at odds with what others say they are seeing or experiencing. Rarely, highly intuitive persons ground as children in believing what they "see" and experience, no matter how at odds they are with others. More often, the highly intuitive person devotes strong mental energies toward the denial of their intuitive feedback. Despite this desperate mechanism, many who would otherwise be pre-disposed toward the recognition of inner truths about reality, end up feeling "weird," and isolated. For such persons, the last 40 years has come as an immense liberation, as intuitive knowledge has come to be valued highly in the general culture.

We are at last at that point where we are far less likely to be devalued if we join our faith to our intuitive understandings, rather than to a set of carefully reasoned beliefs reinforced by one authority or another. We are also at that point where many persons are wondering about their own intuitive, imaginative and creative capacity. People are asking for encouragement in their self-discovery, in the exercise of neglected aspects of themselves. I cannot help but think this is a remarkable period in the widespread evolution of human consciousness.

It is not too much to say that if we do meditate, we may learn how cluttered, obsessive, and negative our thinking is. We may gradually achieve some objectivity about our thinking constructs, and achieve some separateness so we are not stuck with identifying our essential nature with these constructs. My faith construct is that the position we occupy in our consciousness when we can separate *from* our thinking and identify with the observer, is that of Spirit. It is from this place of quiet and peaceful freedom from the dominance of our egos that we are more likely to experience a consciousness of one-ness with Being.

Think, then, of mysticism as an attitude of mind and heart, a turn of the mind away from dependency on proofs, reasoning, and systems of external authority. Think of it as forming a disposition of curiosity, and a longing to be one with the One. Think of it as a willingness to be surprised and to be changed.

The varieties of practices and teachers mystics have found useful appears almost as endless as the number of mystics themselves. Let me illustrate how intensely individualistic the mystical path for learning and expression may be from an experience I had in China.

When I first retired I was most fortunate in being able to join a relatively small group of persons, mostly professionals in the health field, who were going to China to study the practice of qigong and its relationship to Traditional Chinese Medicine. I was already a practitioner of Soaring Crane Qigong, which I had learned from my teacher, Hui-Xian Chen, a lovely woman from Shanghai who taught at the Oriental School of Medicine in Portland, Oregon. There are at least 500 different forms of qigong. The earliest were first created thousands of years ago by shamans, probably from Mongolia, and modeled after the movements of birds and animals. The shamans believed humans needed to be in harmony with nature and its rhythms if they were to survive, stay healthy and be at peace.

The study and practice of qigong is consistent with an inward path toward greater consciousness. Its movements require concentration, attention to balance, and consciousness of energy flows inside and outside the body. To practice qigong is to recognize that when you *think* you are no longer *aware*. Consciousness of energy is a soft achievement. It entails developing the skills of non-thinking and intuition. The movements of any qigong form may be done as a routine, by rote, simply as a physical exercise, but to do so defeats the intention of most forms of qigong, which is to cultivate inner consciousness. A qigong form whizzed through without attention to the inner life appears to an observer as wooden, and oddly lifeless, no matter how energetic it is.

After our study group had arrived for our 14-day stay in Beijing, we took courses in Traditional Chinese Medicine during the day. Most of our lecturers were Taoist or Buddhist. Their language stemmed from their belief that energy forms the metaphysical and scientific basis for health and healing. We lived on a Chinese Air Force base, and our lodgings were quite comfortable. The food, while unusual, especially at breakfast, was healthy. I had brought along my tennis racquet, and every morning I was up at 5:00 or so to hit a tennis ball up against the cement wall of a barracks garage. I was surprised I was never asked to stop, or arrested, by the guards at the nearby gate who watched me hitting.

The Chinese people who worked on the base looked at me with great curiosity as they went up the road and past me, through the gate, and to their work. Perhaps they wondered if I was a very important person to be able to use a barracks garage wall for hitting a tennis ball. The truth is, I had never asked anyone for permission, and thought if it was against the rules, someone would tell me. No one ever did, and when I got back to the states I got to wondering, did the guards not stop me because they assumed nobody would be foolish enough to use the wall of a military garage wall for tennis exercise, unless they had permission from the very top?

One very bright young Chinese man who gave some of his time to the School also had a professional position in electronics. He often assisted students with the language when they needed to make money exchanges in the city. During one of our trips to the city he struck up a conversation. He had heard I was a tennis player, and he told me he was, too. One thing led to another, and on our way back to the school he took me by an indoor tennis court. I asked him if he would like to play, and I reserved and paid for a court for a Friday. I chose that day because I knew there was a lecture I didn't want to attend. And I definitely wanted a tennis match in China!

It was all arranged, but on Thursday the young man came to me, embarrassed, and gave me back my money.

"Master Chen learned we were going to play and she was upset. She said you were a student of Chinese Medicine and that Friday's lecture was part of your spiritual training. She said I had to get your money back."

I felt really badly about this experience, because knowing Master Chen, I suspected she must really have unloaded on this quite innocent young man; yet, I was the one who had arranged our Friday afternoon match. But, the court had been re-assigned, the young man said, and there was nothing to be done. I apologized, and watched all my fantasies go down the drain, about playing this great Chinese tennis player on an indoor court in downtown Beijing! I knew I needed to have a heart to heart talk with Master Chen.

I went to the Friday afternoon lecture I would have missed, and my instincts had been correct; the presenter was a scientist reporting on his experiments with energy, and all his language was technical. Master Chen, ordinarily a very fine translator, was at sea most of the time, and the class could absorb very little. Most of us were frustrated and bored.

Next day I talked with Master Chen:

"I wanted you to know there are two major paths for me these days in my spiritual journey. One is my marriage, and the other is tennis. These are my qigong."

To her immense credit, Master Chen, after initial puzzlement, understood what I was saying: That I did not see playing tennis as frivolous, but as central to the expansion of my spiritual consciousness. Obviously there was an exercise level and a fun level to tennis. But then there were the unexpected ways my consciousness was expanding through increasingly competitive tennis.

I have received, and learned far more about myself in my marriages, particularly in my current and enduring one of 26 years, than I could imagine recording. To be loved for exactly who one is, and for all that one is, requires the eye and heart of the Divine in one's mate. Love is transforming when we are open to its lessons. I have learned more than I could imagine from my children and stepchildren because of the challenges to my nature and my thought forms. Within such a matrix of Spirit it becomes possible for the harder edges of our egos to soften, and access to our hearts to be further opened. It was the relationship path of personal transformation I spoke about with Master Chen. If the marriage part relates to my feminine side, tennis relates to my masculine, with its emphasis on competition, aggressive engagement, skills, body speed, conditioning, and winning.

It must be clear to the reader that my own shift to an inward place for the creative illumination of my faith came about through beginning a practice of daily meditation. Years of personal psychotherapy also turned me radically inward, and freed me from many thought forms that were limiting and actually self-destructive. Possibly because of the preparation of my psychic ground through psychotherapy, I was able to cultivate my consciousness further through the practice of meditation.

The training that influenced and affected me most was Buddhist Vipassana meditation. My chief teacher, among several, was Ruth Denison, a survivor of Russian vengeance in East Germany, where she was at one time a teacher. A few of my more vivid and definitive ecstatic experiences occurred during longer meditation retreats of nine days with Ruth. My capacity to position my mind as an observer of itself became ever sharper during these and similar retreats. My heart soil must have been ready for the seed of Vipassana.

But what of all the cultivation of the soil of my mind and heart that had to come *first*? How much of me had to be disked, plowed up, turned over, dug into? A lot! Very fortunately, once I became a college teacher and a psychotherapist in Oregon I had opportunities for lengthy training groups in Gestalt Therapy and Bioenergetics with exceptional teachers: Joan Endsley and Dr. Tom Munson of the Gestalt Institute of San Diego, Stanley Keleman, of the Center for Energetic Studies in Berkeley, California. These training groups and my extensive personal psychotherapy created furrows for extensive exploration in intuitive and metaphysical studies. Chief of my teachers in these realms were Carolyn Conger and Dr. Brugh Joy. My consciousness expanded in ways often startling, and my faith took on greater breadth and delight.

Some studies and workshops I engaged in didn't "take." No matter how good they were for other students, they didn't fit my nature. I was a flop at a week with Feldenkreis. I was out of synch for a week of shiatsu training. Some trainings didn't accord with my nature, or perhaps with my stage of spiritual evolution. Consciousness of my body sensations, my internal energy system, and how that is connected to all other energy systems, has been crucial to the nature of my consciousness and my faith. Students of inwardness whose nature is different may have chosen other venues for self-learning.

Religious studies were very important and riveting for me in the earliest days of my spiritual journey, before I left California for Oregon, and before I left the ministry. I have fond memories and immense gratitude to the Cincinnati Bible Seminary, where I first studied in my early 20's, and began to learn about the Bible and the particular independent tradition the Church of Christ espoused. I must say it: I would not be the person I am today, or be able to hold the faith that I do, were it not for those remarkable years in what was at that time, a passionate, but quite fundamentalist environment. Those wonderful folk may not be grateful for me, given much of what I am writing in this book, but I am immensely grateful to them. I am grateful, too, for the Stanford Theologian, Alexander Miller, and my subsequent theological study at Andover Newton Theological School in Boston, particularly to theologian Nels F.S. Ferré. These theological studies formed the early stimulus to my spiritual longing, but they would have been incongruent with others' natures.

If you think of yoga, or Tai Chi, or acupuncture, or meditation training, or a tremendous range of body and energy therapies, you will have an idea of some of the options mystics are more likely to choose to train their consciousness in awareness.

What does the mystic tend to say and believe about what she intuits to be a spiritual reality? She sees it as a truth for herself, one that for this moment binds her, whether to a sense of awe, or as a command to speak out about an ethical issue. But she does not see her truth as *the* truth for everyone. The mystic is skeptical of absolutes and claims to absolute truth. This is in marked contrast with those who promote themselves and their visions, who don't hesitate to call their visions Divine Revelation that require unquestioning belief and obedience. These are charismatic individuals who invite the dependency of disciples to support their illusions of grandiosity, whether in religion or politics. This behavior is antithetical, I believe, to a practice of inwardness.

The mystic is basically a very normal person, pursuing a particular, inward path in creating an organic faith, who is wary of making any absolute claims about herself or Being. Mysticism is a surprisingly loose, and at the same time a highly demanding, belief and practice, because it is based on a relationship of love. And love is always larger than law.

Love ultimately breaks out of all limiting forms because it *questions* all forms through its unexpectedness. It is impossible to contain love in any and all known human packaging, because it invigorates the life that exists within these boxes beyond their existing boundaries. This is not to say love is God. It is to say love is the *essence* of God, and that it is love the pilgrim most feels when he has a sense of being one with God.

I don't seek ecstatic experiences, but occasionally I am unexpectedly graced with one. This year, for some reason, there seem to be more such experiences. Let me tell you of one that appeared to come in two parts, on successive days.

It was close to dinnertime, and I don't recall doing anything different than usual walking around the edge of our coffee table, looking into the Catalina mountains, as I often do. But suddenly I felt arrested in my tracks, and stood paralyzed. A surge of energy coursed through my body. I felt it mostly in my solar plexus and then my heart. My head had already felt the pressure of an unknown energy for several days and nights, disturbing my sleep, insistent that I write, then write some more.

Now these energies joined in an instant, and as I looked out the window I saw tile roofs, desert plants in our back yard, chairs, the mountain, dogs next door that were not visible, coyotes also not visible, elephants, hens...all at once, simultaneously. Everything seemed to vibrate, or shimmer, including me. Suddenly I *knew* I belonged to everything! Everything that was, rocks, trees, elephants, dogs, mountains... I belonged to it all. I belonged to God, and the essence of God was in everything that was. I knew this as the reality of the oneness of the entire universe, and tears rolled down my cheeks.

I felt in shock, made my way to the couch and sat down. I simply stared, until my wife asked me if something was the matter. Slowly, as best I could, I told her what had happened. We sat there until she had to go and take care of the beans that were in danger of being overdone.

Take care of those beans! As vivid a mystical experience as you might have, it differs only in degree from every form of our more ordinary life. It is possible to go from one quite dramatic experience to one much less intense, or even mundane. For the mystic life is not carried out only on the occasional ecstatic peaks, but in the valleys as well.

It is good not to take ourselves or particular experiences too seriously, though ecstatic visions may affect us so deeply we are momentarily in a state of awe and shock. Still, the task of a mystic is to permit the blessed vision to flow into all other expressions of life, to bring its joyful energy to all phases of existence. A healthy mysticism hopes to achieve a decent balance between ecstasy and caring for the beans on the stove.

The other mystical vision which fell out of my mind following the first one, had to do with whales. I suddenly fell in love with whales. I mean, one way or another, I seem always to have been where whales were, especially on the Oregon coast; but, while I noticed, I did not make special trips to see the whales make their way to Alaska or anything like that. I have also been somewhat curious about what profound natures they are alleged to have, their ability to communicate with one another. I have read some stories I did not dismiss, but held skeptically at least, of whales apparently playing a part in the saving of swimmers at sea. Yes, I also knew some human beings felt a great personal affinity with whales, but I did not. They were just one more large thing in the ocean.

My ecstatic vision of whales was that they, of all creatures, save possibly the elephant, are most conscious of their oneness with Being, and with all manifestations of Being. They are, in that sense, the most advanced of all earth's pilgrims. In my moment of feeling I belonged to everything, I thought of the whale, who intuits he belongs to everything, and he does. In the surrounding of the sea, when not endangered by humans, the whale seems playful, demonstrative, and welcomes them. At one with the great waters, all its creatures, and each of its elements, he is at one with humans of heart as well.

I had a new take on the tale of Moby Dick, where there is this ferocious struggle between a whaling captain and a great whale. I came to see the novel by Melville not just as a classic sea adventure story, but as a metaphor for the ego's drive to kill Spirit. If we do not comprehend our oneness with all that is, how shall we not want to control, overpower, overuse, and kill a great many manifestations of that oneness, whether trees or animals or whales?

Mystics often find themselves at odds with policies and authority aligned with greed or a need for power. It may be possible to hide from moral confrontations, oddly, within a church, especially if there's an assumption of many of its members that the church "should not meddle in politics." The church may be at times an unwieldy sword of the Spirit. Mystics do not have that kind of refuge. They *must* contend with the quiet urgings of Being within themselves every day. They, as Thoreau once said, are compelled to listen to a different drummer.

CHAPTER 10

Channeling as a Mystical Practice

Sooner or later the pilgrim who has made his inner life his laboratory for intuitive learning is likely to explore the phenomenon of channeling. Channeling is a belief there are non-material entities available to human consciousness who, under the right conditions, will be vehicles for a wisdom larger than our own. This wisdom is believed to be less bound by our space and time dimensions because the agents for channeling inhabit more advanced planes in the universe.

I became convinced of the legitimacy of some channeled wisdom well over 30 years ago. I have a way of testing other plane revelation for its authenticity that satisfies me sufficiently to believe it is possible, without having to make any claims of absolute truth or divine authority for it. My method rests on an accumulation of 40 years of training in body-mind therapy and consciousness. It relies on a kind of lie-truth detector in my system, particularly in the belly and forehead, that apparently combines an energetic charge in those areas with intuitive vision, and registers that phenomenon in my larger mind.

This may sound too mysterious for many readers to be considered a reliable criterion of truth, but it is a criterion I have found works best for me, and a method that bypasses, in my opinion, many thinking conformities that automatically exclude the possibility of wisdom from other planes. I believe an attention to interior "hits" about truth promotes a more open mind to phenomena often dismissed by those who reject intuitive access to truth. It is the same old saw, if you can't prove it rationally or scientifically, then it doesn't exist. If you can't see spirit guides, sometimes called guardian angels, then they must not exist.

Consistent with my confidence in inner testing, and the larger curiosity of my basic nature, I frequently explored what is known as channeling. I paid for sessions with a variety of "psychics" who claimed to channel other entities. I got referrals from our common underground of friends, other psychotherapists, and clients who were known to be reliable persons on the advancing edge of psychic exploration. I went because I was curious, and didn't want to close down a possible source of wisdom for my spiritual path. Invariably, the psychics who were recommended to me as "authentic" were not publicly advertised figures. They tended to be relatively obscure and quite ordinary human beings with an unusual gift: they apparently could communicate with entities from another dimension.

I read a wide range of books that were said to be channeled, a few dating from the early part of the last century. I read authors who varied widely in their experience and explanation of "Spirit Guides," sometimes referred to as "Guardian Angels." What they did agree on was that these were entities appointed by the Divine to assist us, seen or unseen, on our journey of consciousness.

I found an unusual diversity of trance and speaking styles among psychics, but a similarity of language in writing style that claimed to record channeled wisdom. The psychics I happened to visit, without exception dropped into a trance state and adopted voices very different from their own to channel a particular entity. Despite numerous experiences, I never failed to be startled by the strangeness of the tone, inflections, and rhythms of these "other plane" voices.

Since in any session with a psychic who channeled I had questions I wanted to ask that were important to my personal and/or spiritual life, I had a good opportunity to weigh the validity and depth of the information I received. The usefulness of information I received was helpful in some instances and not relevant in others. But even in the helpful sessions, the "wisdom" was so generalized that I felt it could have been applicable to anyone. Did I conclude there *was* an entity channeling answers to the questions I had brought to these sessions? I was agnostic. Not enough data to register on my inner truth detector. Did I conclude the psychic herself (or himself) believed that she was channeling an entity? Yes, she had a self-belief in her honesty in this process, and a belief she was helping people. There was no way I could render an opinion as to the amount of self-deception that may have been involved in the confidence these folks had in their beliefs. But I do believe they were personally good people, and I believe they sincerely wanted to help me.

The books and articles were another matter. Without exception they shared a tonality, an eerie kind of distance, as if they were, indeed, speaking from another plane. I also made a judgment about which ones were "best," and which were rather pedestrian, or too esoteric on the other hand. There were many 'best ones,' and I found them stimulating, appealing to the deepest elements of my own nature, and my truth register said "yes!" These people are channeling entities from a wiser dimension than our own.

When I read the best articles or books it was as if I felt instantly in the company of a peaceful, compassionate, and wise community of entities. The experience was invariably inspiring. I seem now to know the way in which these entities employ our language. They speak directly, with an absence of emotional tone, and the writing by the one channeling at its best exhibits few or no ego intrusions or attention to ordinary requirements of writing style. I recall one channeled article on psychotherapy that astounded me in its deep insights and fresh vision about the therapeutic process. The person channeling, a psychotherapist herself, was equally astounded to have received such advanced wisdom about a field she had been in for many years. Fortunately she had the session printed verbatim and issued it as pamphlet, which I still have— somewhere.

I have returned to one or two books many times over the years because their channeled wisdom continues to find a home in my own nature. My favorite, "The Starseed Transmissions," is so direct and simple, and at the same time so wise. The spiritual entity is named Raphael, and his wisdom teachings were received and compiled by Kenneth X. Carey. Carey appears to think of himself as a quite ordinary person. He lived in Missouri when this late '80's book was published.

It is wonderful to have so many questions about channeling. It suggests our own inner wisdom can afford an openness to spiritual truths that can be coupled with healthy agnosticism. The heart is just such a place, possessed of a kind of joyful innocence, yet piercing in its perception of what is true, false, or something else. If you have a predisposition toward authenticity, and hold to your own counsel, rather than giving it away to others, you have nothing to fear from explorations of channeling. It is one more adventure possible to you on your spiritual journey. Similar to many other adventures, some flow into our consciousness to enlarge it, others connect with us less, and do not.

One of my inner adventures became a great contributor to an enlarged faith and consciousness. I began to explore possible contact with what, or who, might be my own Spirit Guide, since I had pretty much come to believe that everyone had one. So, I set to work in my inner lab. First, I asked if he (I had already presumed if there were such things as Spirit Guides, and that if they emanated from another dimension, they would likely not have a gender. My designation, "he," was a concession to my own gender.) would be willing to talk with me. He immediately said he was. So we began.

Strangely, I can't seem to capture the time period when I had my first encounters with my Spirit Guide. At first I thought it was during a month in Israel, more specifically during a two-week period in Jerusalem. That particular span of time was very powerful and affecting energetically. I do know we had very significant exchanges during that time late in 1999. But when I looked through some of my old journals and papers, I discovered exchanges between me and my Spirit Guide as early as 1991. In any event, I found it useful to personalize my Spirit Guide, though for some reason I didn't want to ask him if he had a name; so, I just called him S.G., and visualized him like a Walter Winchell character, with a felt hat tilted to one side of his head, and a cigar hanging from his mouth.

Over the years I asked S.G. to speak with me on an average of once a week. Sometimes, if my questions were more pressing, I would talk with S.G. several times in one week. During other periods we could go for an entire month without visiting. Every single encounter was valuable and insightful. Most contained genuine surprises of unexpected advice or statements about metaphysical truths. His teasing humor about my seriousness was invariably accurate, funny, and clearly accepting. He faced me into many aspects of my character and personality in the most direct, yet gentle, way I could ever imagine. And because of what he said and how he did it, it was impossible to feel defensive, or for my ego to get out of joint. Consequently, I could position myself better after our sessions to change what I needed to. As S.G. often said, "Sure, change. Why not? Isn't that what life is all about? But slowly, kid, slowly. Be patient with yourself."

I would describe S.G.'s responses to my questions, and his advice, as clear, direct, authentic to my limited experience, and realistic within the framework of my history and time dimension. He was gently confronting and very, very wise. Let me give you another example of why I came to trust S.G. so much.

I had been puzzled about claims to absolute truth some well-known channelers were making for transmitted information. While I respected S.G. enormously, and was so grateful for all he had given me, never once did I automatically assume that everything he said could be of an absolute character, normative for me and all other earthly beings. But, since others did think their entity revelations were absolute, I decided to take the question to S.G. himself. I asked him,

"Do you have any limitations yourself?"

"Of course," he replied

"Does that mean we should not necessarily take as absolute and binding everything you say?" I asked.

"You have never heard me make such a claim, and it could not possibly be true. Though I occupy a more advanced dimension than your own, I, too, have truths I still must learn, and am evolving in the universe."

"Then what is the place you occupy?" I queried.

"A valued place, I hope. That you will receive what I tell you with gratitude, just as I offer it to you as a gift. But it is a gift from a being also limited in ways sometimes clear to me, and at other times unclear to me. So receive the gift and make use of it, but do not treat what I say as absolute truth, not subject to error, for it is not."

"Thank you, S.G."

"Don't mention it." (and he smiles)

I can't imagine entities (if they are formed like S.G.) whose confidence in their wisdom is obviously linked to humility about their limitations, making claims to speak absolutely—unless they are fallen angels intent on seduction and deception? Therefore, if an alleged entity claims absolute cosmic knowledge, I am forced to conclude the person who channels that entity has projected his or her own need for absolute truth onto that entity. I think claims to absolute cosmic knowledge indulge in a dangerous self-deception, because such claims cannot help but foster an outbreak of dependency and psychic cultism within some readers or listeners who *want* to believe they can have direct access to absolute truth. I scratch my head and have a puzzled frown. This need to believe we know something *absolutely* must originate as a very powerful drive in human nature.

I was reading along in a very popular psychological-metaphysical book a couple of years ago when I realized, from the tonality of the sentence structure, that the author was recording channeled material as if it were his own creation. He was neither acknowledging an entity voice nor claiming the words he was typing were channeled. That, in itself, was suspect; but what really set me off was the inherent claim his writing made to absolute knowledge about metaphysical realities. You would recognize the name of the author of the book, if I said it, for he is a most charming, and I think good, person, who has appeared on major television programs. But, in his failure to acknowledge much of his material is channeled, and in refusing to question the finality and authority of its language, the good person and good writer is unethical in my view. He will sell a lot of books, but I think at considerable cost to the truth. I trust S.G. when he warns of any channeled claims for absolute truth. I think this is one more indication of how the general population hungers for charismatic authority and how easily it is seduced by hunger for an authoritative spiritual voice outside themselves.

There is a perfectly respectable argument that entities are unacknowledged aspects of our own deeper wisdom nature. In short, they are disowned projections of our own creativity and imagination. It is not what I believe, but it is an interesting theory which in many ways correlates well with other parts of this book. I happen to like more magical views, and am drawn to the idea of angels who care for us and try to awaken us to greater consciousness. As I said, I like visualizing S.G. as a Walter Winchell kind of character, sardonic, gently confronting, all those characteristics that I find really interesting and supportive in my journey. For now I am not interested in the more abstract and "cool" theory he is a projection of myself. Perhaps someday I will think otherwise, but for now I am perfectly happy to see S.G. as an advanced helper and teacher on my behalf.

My complaint about the author and book I refer to anonymously is that there is no attempt to address this dilemma at all. The writing just goes on without any acknowledgement of the likelihood it is channeled material, without, in fact, any discussion of the fascinating metaphysical and mystical issue of channeling.

This leads me to another most interesting theory about channeling and those who do it. Because channeling is often a powerful energetic and spiritual experience for a pilgrim, or mystic, it can become as addictive as a drug. One can be addicted to channeling because of the "high," and not realize one's ego has really taken over the process. Indeed, this may be one source for the grandiose claims some who channel make for the metaphysical and personal information they claim to receive.

Another way of looking at this is to use a Buddhist frame of reference and suggest some who channel become "attached" to this one thought form, sometimes dangerously for their own spiritual life.

I was never sure whether my conversations with S.G. should remain a private matter, or whether, under certain circumstances, I could share them with others. On one occasion I shared an S.G. conversation with my daughters, and I often did with my wife. Those ventures seemed permissible, within a respect for the Sacred. About more public sharing I had reservations, and was particularly worried over the ease with which I felt my ego needs could attach themselves to my conversations with S.G. if I became public with S.G.'s wisdom.

An occasion soon developed that would address my interest in having others experience S.G.'s wisdom, as well as my fear of my ego intrusions into what I considered a sacred process. I had been a member of a men's group for two or three years, and over time we shared many experiences. One was the nature of our spiritual quests. I spoke of my experiences with a spirit guide as an important aspect of my spiritual life. One of the men in the group wondered if S.G. would be willing to talk with the men's group. So the issue of going public with my spirit guide was on the table. I told the man I would find out. What follows is a transcript of my subsequent conversation with S.G. about his speaking with my men's group, recorded in January of the year 2000.

Don: One of the men in my men's group wonders if you would be willing to talk with the group, or individuals in the group?

SG. Yes, but the sacredness, and in some ways, fragility, of *our* relationship must be respected and kept intact.

D. The men, or any one of them, could threaten my contact with you?

SG. Think of the manner of my communication, link, with you as a tube, comprised of material which is an energy frequency, or pace of vibration, which is right at that place (though it is not really a location, because it is more like an invisible line) where one leaves eternity, or timelessness, and enters *your* dimension of time and space. So it is both permeable and impermeable. It participates in both states of Being.

D. Continue.

SG. So, if there are too many states of consciousness that are fixated, attached rigidly, to the permeable, to time and space, *that* consciousness will arrest or interfere with the vibrational frequency necessary for us to have communication. It is like a radio message, or wave, being broken up.

D. Continue.

SG. So nothing "bad" would happen. It would merely mean the contact with me and the men, or ones among the men, could be hindered, perhaps even distorted.

D. The state of consciousness of these men is unknown to me. I don't know what they will bring.

SG. Sure, no problem. I just wanted you to know there could be interferences and breakups of my words and contact.

D. What would happen? Nothing to say, or garbled words?

SG. *Plenty* to say, especially to a group that large, each with his own Spirit Guide. It is just that I would not be able to *say* it. Human consciousness, or forms of it, can exclude me and my dimension of being from their dimension of reality. So, the contact is broken, nothing can get through.

D. Even with the help of their spirit guides?

SG. All of us (spirit guides) are restricted by the limitations of human consciousness. It is not that we are not present; sometimes, perhaps often, humans experience another dimension by intuition and/or in ways they can only call mystery, but, they are fearful of making us a constant in their lives. Their egos are resistant to something so boundless and barely imaginable, except to the heart and intuition.

D. Thank you. As I understand it, you are willing to meet or speak with the men, but you are warning me of what may become limitations.

SG. Yes

D. Could there be other problems?

SG. No, unless it might be the interferences of your own ego, what you call, "self-consciousness." If there is any embarrassment over me and my reality in your life, that will become a vibrational interference.

D. Do I have to be careful of my own motivations, or secondary gains...like I get to "show you off," and secondarily get attention for that?

SG. The possibility cannot be excluded, but I will help you with that issue, work with you. It is a core issue for any human being who makes public his or her conversations with "The Other." How do you keep from contaminating the Incarnational Word?

There was a bit more to our conversation, but what is here may be enough to portray my concern about "going public" with S.G. As it turned out, the problem solved itself. I told the men S.G. had agreed to meet and speak with them, if they wished, and after telling them S.G.'s response, not a single man ever brought up the subject again. No one asked if we could plan for a session with S.G. present. I think I will leave any interpretations of this turn of events up to my readers. Frankly, I was more relieved than puzzled, and more puzzled than disappointed!

My reporting of a portion of this conversation with S.G. is the first public writing I have done about channeling, other than to my wife, once to my children, and once to a very dear friend. It is S.G.'s first public appearance in print.

In 2005, S.G. stopped appearing for conversations. Several times during meditation, I positioned my consciousness to welcome him, and on one occasion even asked him to appear. But S.G. did not appear. I reflected on this for several weeks. I came to believe it was his final teaching to me, a wisdom he had left. He did not want me dependent on him either. He wanted me to trust my own wisdom and answer my own questions. This made sense to me, because in the last several meetings with S.G., when I had asked him important questions, I was aware I was forming surprisingly articulate and unexpected answers to my questions before S.G. could answer. I'm sure he was aware I had internalized a faster vibrational band of consciousness into my nature. The visualization of a Spirit Guide separate from myself was dissolving—that form was yielding to new forms of imaginative creativity inhabiting my heart, mind and body.

Is my interpretation of the departure of S.G. an accurate one? Who can know for certain? But, I do know that my understanding of his absence correlates with much of what I have come to believe and written of in this book.

Will I meet S.G. again for conversations, ever? It's possible. He spoke briefly with me when I asked him to, after I was terribly confused and depressed after my serious surgery. I may need my familiar friend and guide again, need his simple but wise way of thinking. I may need his teasing humor if I become too serious. I am so fond of him. My heart and eyes fill. Maybe for that reason alone I may one day ask him back, just to visit on some park bench.

I have not forgotten his message: don't become too attached to the messenger. It is what the messenger reveals to you about *who you are* that is important.

> You are one with the One,
>
> and you must live from your heart.

CHAPTER 11

If You Are God

When Barbara Walters interviewed the Dalai Lama, she asked him if he was God, he blurted out, "Oh heavens no!"

How is it, then, that a recent consciousness has arisen within me that I *am* God? It seems ridiculous and preposterous! To own that edges my ego into embarrassment. Yet, in my deepest non-ego consciousness, I cannot deny I am God.

Can I square the report of my consciousness with the Dalai Lama's surprised but spontaneous denial he was God? No, I can't. Not reasonably. Here is this remarkably humble man from Tibet, revered throughout the world, who seems disinterested in putting forth a pious image. He strikes me as aversive to claiming knowledge or authority. He clearly is a man who is excited about learning, and curious about science and the world he inhabits. He enjoys his dialogues with young people, and they seem drawn instinctively to him, perhaps because he has a delightful sense of humor. Without claims or posturing, the Dalai Lama radiates a spirit that affects all of us, and some of my friends deeply.

On the other hand, I can't deny a dawning consciousness that I am God. I imagined an interview I could have with someone.

Q. Do you think you are God?

D. No. I don't *think* that I am God. It is an *awareness* I am God.

Q. But *are* you God?

D. If the emphasis of your question falls on *God*, and not the *you*, in your question, yes, I am God.

Q. Do you claim to be God?

D. To be honest, I invited you to ask that question before we began our interview. I needed to clarify exactly, that I don't *claim* to be God. Wouldn't that separate me from you, or all other beings, as if I were different from them? Wouldn't it create a mind set in them that I had authority, even Divine Authority, to make claims upon them? If I made a *claim* I was God, wouldn't this create a mind set of awe and possible dependency on my personality and words? Now, you are supposed to say, "Yes."

We must have a sense of humor about God-consciousness or we will not understand we are the same, you and I, the one who interviews and the one who replies, the one who writes and the one who reads.

That is the best I can do with this absurd dilemma of hearing the Dalai Lama deny he is God and knowing I *cannot* deny I am God, even if it exposes me to the horror and embarrassment of my ego.

One day a realization *you* are God may arise from your conscious-ness. Perhaps it already has. You may need to accept that your consciousness has momentarily outwitted or outstripped your ego. You are no longer exclusively controlled by it. An essence of Being has arisen to your awareness like a fluttering butterfly touching a flower, or like an aroma of lavender. Your commitment to a live faith has fertilized your toleration for a consciousness you have never dared to imagine.

Don't let your grasp of such an astounding reality freak you out. It is a fleeting and periodic consciousness piece set among many other pieces. But it *is* the centerpiece. Obviously, most of the time and in most ways, you are *not* God. But you sense that in all the ways you are *not* God, in *those* ways the pieces will be *permeated* by the Centerpiece energies if you permit and encourage it to be so through your faith.

My experience so far teaches me that to the degree I *am* conscious I am God, and don't let my ego mess around with that consciousness, I think *about* God less. I just go about my business with an assumption of Presence, not even very concerned about how unpredictably that Presence may affect, bless, challenge, or change me, until either I become aware a change is underway or someone else recognizes it. I have fewer fixed definitions or views of *who* and *what* God might be, both of which make God an object rather than a subject. I believe I am more open to what and who God wants to create in and of me, including my imagination and faith. I sometimes have the strange thought that God is creating and recreating Himself in me, in all beings, in all of His creation. Wow! That's a hard one to take in!

I am coming to believe an imaginative faith lets go of "God" and gives Him the freedom to *be*, including Being in us, and gives *us* the freedom to *be*. My guess is that the Dalai Lama's spacious faith is what gives *him* the freedom to *be*, what appears to be his freedom to delight in life, and to engage it with his mind and heart without the need for ego trappings of image and authority. As I am writing in this moment,

I realize my comments resemble much of what I have written about "letting go of Jesus," letting go of external authority objects so we free up compressed energies and a fixed faith, liberate them to create a vital personal faith.

There is a part of me that sometimes becomes frightened of a consciousness that I am God. My thinking ego associates such consciousness with delusions of grandeur, with self-deception, with naivety, and yes, with stupidity. Here we are, so mortal we don't even know if our bodies will hold together for another year, let alone another decade. We live on a space-time continuum, we have obvious limitations of skill, intelligence and insight. Emotionally we struggle with the same conflicts most people do. I worry what people will think of me, that I'm nuts, that I have my head in the clouds, or that I am simply an arrogant ass. I've always feared criticism. But for a long time I have had no choice, had to stay true to myself, and to my beliefs and visions. Ultimately, we all have to learn to live with how we're put together. So if you run into me, smile, and ask me if I am God, because you've read this book. You'll know I'll smile back at the absurdity of it all, and we'll both have a good laugh. Faith is a *funny thing*. Well, at least a curious thing.

The other day on public radio I was listening to a scientist who also has an advanced degree in philosophy. He was saying that it may become possible at some point for one human being to create a parallel universe through his or her creative imagination. He said it was not impossible theoretically. This vision is very close to how I am understanding faith as an organic, imaginative process that creates possibilities. All kinds of possibilities, not only the transformation of our bodies and brains, or a teddy bear's eyes and molecular structure, but transformations of political and religious structures and cultural attitudes. *We may be evolving and creating* a *faith that confronts us with the sacred responsibility for creating* a *God who is worthy of our faith.* This is the mind-blowing paradox I am presenting, that in our evolution of consciousness, we become aware we are God creating the God who creates us!

The first time I realized the deep, persuasive truth of the statement, "I am God," I didn't feel it as a *claim* to be God. Claims have to do with ownership, separation, distance, and power. It was a simple statement that seemed to have no connection with my ego whatsoever. Maybe my ego was asleep. I felt no aversion, at least in that moment, to the statement. I did feel a deep sense of peace. I heard a comment, as if were a wry commentary from my Spirit Guide, S.G.

"So? So you are God, so what? No big deal. Everybody is, they just don't know it yet."

We know so much about the level of consciousness that shouts we are *not* God! Let me tell you the ways! Or ask my wife, who knows my humanness so well and yet loves me into immense gratitude that we found one another. But how much do we know of that level of consciousness where we may *begin* to comprehend we *are* God? Isn't that worth exploring unemotionally, but with our hearts and our creative imagination? We may have to park our egos somewhere, as in a dark parking lot where they can't see us and are likely to fall asleep. But it's exciting, the human possibilities for exploring inner space!

If the consciousness I have somewhat fearfully, and yet honestly described, should come upon you, you're likely to feel very, very humbled, as if some kind of accident, or aberration has just occurred. Who knows, maybe I have a brain tumor! I actually wondered that, briefly, being unable to account for how this new vision of consciousness came upon me. I could have been washing dishes the first time it happened, or watching "House" on television. The vision had probably been forming for some time, germinating as it were, in my consciousness. The vision of God-ness hasn't made my life any different so far as I can see, except that I feel more liberated than ever to enjoy everything I do, enjoy my tennis game, my writing, the people we know, my family. It hasn't been like lightning struck our house, or me in particular. I'm still the same old guy who complains about sinuses, allergies, and how travel has become so much more complicated than it used to be.

I hope you *do* catch a glimpse of who you are in your essential being, and that you are able to say, "I am *that*." I'm prejudiced enough to believe such a vision will bring a smile to your face, and fill your life with confidence and hope. I hope, too, that you don't feel any need to walk outside and tell everybody, or even anybody, about it. After all, the experience is just one more thing in your journey of faith. There's still the shopping to do, maybe take the dog for a walk. Look, he's wagging his tail! Realizing you are God is pretty important, but it *is* just one more thing, like smiling during a walk when you see an ocotillo in bloom.

I don't have any expectations of myself because of this new consciousness. It's still the same wrinkled face, same pony tail, looking back at me from the mirror. Same wobbling walk when I go outside to retrieve the morning newspaper. Same smile when I think of my wife and kids. Same heart-skip when I think of good friends.

I'm not under any obligation to be "wise," nor will you be because you have a vision of the sacred within yourself. Hindus are easily at home with this vision of being one with God. Westerners like us are going to have to get used to it. If someone *said* I was wise, I'd say, " I doubt it. Or at least not intentionally, and not very often." And I would not just be trying to be modest or humble. I would mean it. I'm basically still a seeker, and it's probable there will be more inner discoveries that fit my nature and the organic character of my faith if I have more years left to me to explore.

I encourage my readers to take charge of their lives and the character of their faith. Probably you already are, or you would not be reading this book! Especially in our time we need a creative change of inner chemistry far more than we need a compulsive morality driven by the fear of an angry God who may send us to hell because we don't believe the right articles of faith. The degree to which we get stuck in rigid, negative thinking, attitudes and habits, may relate directly to the constraints our faith has placed on the definition of the God we have created.

We have sometimes reversed, I think, how spiritual reality works. We may believe if we shape up and improve our lives, God will approve, and then we will feel forgiven and accepted. In traditional religious frameworks, we will have eternal life. But the dynamic process of human transformation, I believe, works the other way around: when we have the courage, audacity, and imagination to create a larger God, one who can fully and generously inhabit the culture of our souls, I believe we will become lighter, happier, and more generous toward other beings. We will *experience* our eternal nature through our temporal engagement. My only job is to go about my business.

It is a very big step to endow our natures with Divinity. But it has to be done. How else shall we have the deepest respect for our creative intelligence and how to use it? How else shall we think of ourselves as driven by more than our needs, egocentric control and survival? How else will we be able to escape the confining box of illusions we employ to deny our hulking mortality? How else will we have the courage to create and recreate a vital personal faith?

There may be another way to put it. If we are going to have illusions about ourselves, why not create generous illusions, kind illusions. Why not strive to create a reality that possesses compassion and dignity? If it is too frightening to think of yourself as God, then why not think of yourself as a participant in the Essence of God, drawing upon the Divine energies and wisdom? At least attempt to accept the possibility there is some part of you that is larger than your habits, drives, prejudices and ego. There is some part of you that participates in timelessness, beyond aging and mortality.

Are we still on the same page, even if not with the same beliefs? Then let me continue. For those ready to believe that in their deepest essence they are one with God, whatever their egos may be about, or their fading bodies, here is what I wish to say:

If it is likely, or at least possible, you *are* the Creator, then please respect *what* it is you create. Create attitudes of respect for the thinking of others. Our world has a history of some people wanting to *kill* other people because they differ in their thinking, or their faith, particularly in how they think about God .The great religions of the world, when held captive by raging men and women entranced with their own power, have been used to justify beheadings, burnings at the stake, hangings, and assassinations, all in the name of God's (substitute Jehovah, Allah, Shiva) will.

Not only must we create a *god* worthy of our respect and love, but we must create *thinking, attitudes* and *behaviors* worthy of the god we want to create! If you discover your habitual mind to be rattling along with hostility, grudges, guilt, and expectations of bad things happening to you, you don't have to put up with this way of thinking, you know. You can create useful defenses against negativity toward others and yourself. If you are God the Creator, you have great powers to create sanctuaries for yourself where you can rest from the exhaustion of your past traumas, and from your own assaults on yourself. If you are God, be as kind toward yourself as you would want God to be toward you. Be as kind to others as you would want God to be toward you. It is the Creator God who takes delight in your becoming an increasingly compassionate and decent human being. This is the God whom it is your opportunity to create, the One who supports and encourages your very best, not *so* God can love you, but because *you* have created a God who *does* love you.

I wish you the attendant blessings of your special path, and the illuminations you receive from a creative, imaginative, and vital faith.

CHAPTER 12

The Advantages of Aging

When I first visited China as a part of a qigong study group 20 years ago, one of my delights was finding sizable gatherings of Chinese men and women engaging in various forms of qigong early in the morning. Most met in spacious parks to do their various and beautiful sequences. They might number as few as 15 or as many as 200. There were other gatherings held in empty spaces near fields of crops, or occasionally in an inconspicuous courtyard. In most gatherings women outnumbered men in the groups, though often an older man would be guiding the sequences.

During a visit to one of Beijing's best known parks, a few of us cut out with our bus driver shortly after we had all completed a glorious experience of doing our most familiar qigong form, "Soaring Crane." What had made our practice that morning memorable, aside from our being 20 students of qigong who were obviously Caucasian, was finding ourselves by the end of our practice surrounded by 20 or more young Chinese men and women, all taking our pictures!

The word had spread rapidly. I imagine they were especially impressed by our leader for the practice that morning, an accomplished young American woman, just 20 years old, who stood over six feet tall, slender, and as graceful a person as you could imagine. We also knew her to be an advanced martial arts practitioner, as well as a second year student of Chinese Medicine.

After five of us had split from the major group to return a more interesting way back to the bus, I lagged behind at one place. I became fascinated by a group of 40 persons, almost all women, practicing a form of qigong I hadn't seen. It was very graceful, and I found myself joining their motions. They had their backs to me and were far enough away so I felt I could copy their moves without disturbing their concentration and rhythms. I had imitated several moves within one sequence, awkwardly, but genuinely affected. As I was bending down, imitating the group's circling of arms and hands, I suddenly realized a Chinese woman was right next to me, making the same motions. How had she noticed me? How had I *not* seen or heard her, until she appeared like a ghost?

When the woman recognized I had seen her, she smiled as she moved, clearly pleased I had joined the group in their morning qigong, and was assisting me in learning the sequences of their practice. Though I was embarrassed, and immediately less fluid than I had been, supposedly inconspicuous, I was also very warmed by her presence. I continued to join her moves until I noticed my little bus driver group had left me behind! I joined my hands and bowed to her, and pointed to where I had to go. She smiled as I stood up, and gave a little wave of her hand as I started to leave. As I went into a little trot, I took one more look back, and was startled and touched to see that every single person from the qigong group was standing and facing my way, waving. I waved back, kept running, and my heart filled.

How does the Beijing park experience relate to the possible advantages of aging? I think our hearts may be opening more. Not only were most of those in the Qigong gathering I observed women, but they were older. I would guess 80% were past the child-raising and hard-working periods of their lives, and at last they had some leisure. And I was older, older than anyone in my qigong overseas study group. My heart was probably more prepared for many touching experiences in China than it would have been when I was younger. I wrote some of my best poetry in Beijing, so my heart experiences also vitalized my imagination and creativity.

In Beijing parks men, especially older men, sought greater enlightenment, health and longevity through the practice of qigong. On one occasion I was off by myself in a park, and as I made my way through some rocks I unexpectedly found myself in a quiet space among the boulders with five or six older Chinese men. They were obviously engaged in a spirited discussion, about, I suspect, some aspect of their own qigong practice.

I found other practices of the older men in the Beijing parks equally fascinating. During the bus-driver led jaunt of the five of us, he gave us time to take in a view of a very large gathering of older Chinese men who had brought their birds and bird cages to a little plaza. They were talking animatedly, pointing to their little birds, or holding up their cages, sharing I would imagine where they had found their birds, sounds they made, what feed they gave to them, and so on. It was their communion, and the time they had to participate in this "community of the bird cages" that was more than just quaint, and more than unusual. Their communion, their shared connection with one another in their aging was also touching. As I write this, I am reminded of a good friend of mine who said some time back,

"Well, I have enjoyed the years and variety of my work. I have enjoyed making enough money to retire, and now I want to use the last years of my life to pursue the questions and life of the Spirit."

He and I have had many stimulating discussions, beneficial to each of us, since he is of a more scientific and rational bent than I. It seems to me one of the advantages of aging is that we have leisure time to devote to what we may not have done before, and among these is nourishing the spirit, cultivating communion.

Many persons turning 60 are prone to ask the larger questions about life that they either didn't have the time for previously, or may not even have thought of. That they may be less satisfied with traditional answers does not surprise me. In the face of our mortality, we want to go right to the heart of our deepest longings and instincts for what's real and enduring. One's personal faith may take on its greatest spurt, and result in its most profound authenticity, in the last 20 or 30 years of our lives. That is, if our minds and hearts are really open. If they are not, we shall more likely become increasingly terrified and unaccountably angry, and look to others, such as the government, or our children, to give us what they really cannot, an adequate reason for living, and for joy, as we grow older.

I don't have prescriptions for other folk in how to make the best use of their last 20 or 30 years. In this book I have told you of experiences that either drew me to a path or occurred on a path I was walking at the time. The path each of us does best is our own, the one we recognize is for *us* because of the energy it holds, the gravitational pull on our being. That path, once taken, will begin to define itself as we take one step at a time. A significant step is to say "yes!" to aging, rather than living in denial we are getting older and hating it.

I am fortunate, in my view, to have discovered that while my first "aging" decade has reduced my energy, and I must husband my energy wisely, this decade has also accelerated my consciousness. My inner vision seems clearer, and the curtain between this plane and another sometimes appears very thin indeed! It is so paradoxical for my body to be diminishing and my physical pace slowing, while my creativity feels liberated, compared with life at say 30, 40, or 50. My enthusiasms for life are as large as ever. They just have to be experienced and expressed somewhat less exuberantly, and in a smaller geographical and social arena. As I age, I find myself taking more responsibility for creating fresh and vital faith forms.

In truth, I don't like a lot of things about aging. Who does? I don't like fading. Fading hearing, fading eyesight, fading stamina, fading skills, fading sexuality, fading competitive fire on the tennis court. We all have our lists of what we don't like about aging. But there's always *what's left*. Sometimes I think our capacity for pleasure is as limited as our stomachs are for holding a comfortable amount of food. Try to eat more and we suffer. Try to jam too much "pleasure" in and we get a pleasure-ache. In my experience, when I look at people who are seeing much of who they were fade, it startles me. Yet, over and over again, they are the lovely beings who have taught me: how much pleasure they take in *what's left*. I sometimes—no, often—think I enjoy life now more than I ever have. Until now, as I write, I don't believe I stopped to think about why that might be so. I believe it *is* because I take so much pleasure in what is left to me. *Left* of my energy and how carefully I must use it, *left* of my skills on the tennis court, *left* of the years or months I will have with my wife, or my children, our friends, my buddies on the court. Everything takes on an almost intrinsic beauty of its own. Some would say a surreal beauty because nothing resembles it from all our preceding years. So maybe I cannot have a gourmet life any longer, but I can take great pleasure in how much I enjoy each bite of what I do have of life. And seriously? I doubt that younger people than I enjoy *life* that much more than I do. This, I believe, happens for most of us who are open to aging and the gifts of consciousness it can bring to us, even as we are fading. If it is our illusion, it is a pretty good one! It is pretty fair art we are creating in our last years.

In the rest of this chapter on "The Advantages of Aging," I will share some fairly unusual advantages I have discovered in getting older. Perks that take us past AARP. I have liked some of the surprises of aging.

But first, I want to bitch a little. I want to unleash my agnostic dog and let him bark some. I eventually get irritated, and weary, of articles that fairly burst with pictures of 65 year old latter day adolescents who apparently can play all day and all night, and yet wear only broad smiles the next morning. And very, very few wrinkles! I get irritated with articles that contend retirement can blossom with the flowers of sexual abandonment, and that cite obscure statistics to "prove" it. Enough of that. Some of these articles have something to sell. It can be a new pill on the market. It can be an exercise machine. It can be a self-help book. Whatever. But its market is an aging population affected by their fear of aging and death. Other articles seem more to be written by authors who have not come to terms with their own aging faces and bodies, and who apparently have no models to teach them about the *gifts* of aging. They are so frightened of the theft of their youth they cannot believe there can be gifts: what there is to be learned from *aging*, or how they might come to enjoy it. But, then, if you are about to retire, who wants to hear about surgeries or depression, to name two dark-side intruders into our aging years?

Seniors, upon first reading exclusively slanted young-forever articles, may wonder if there is something drastically wrong with them. But then, their agnostic side, and their sense of humor, reassures them they are not "odd," or missing something. They rightly, I think, conclude that love, for the aging, more often refers to tender companionship and mutual respect, than it does acrobatic sex. They understand aging as a period in which to support one another's creativity and growth, and depression and grieving as normal experiences in a community of the aging.

I also have troubles with articles consisting only of a string of "heroic" stories for the aging. You know the ones: "Eighty-five-year-old woman writes successful novel." "Ninety year old man runs 100 yard dash." I celebrate these folks, and I cheer for anyone who is aging and who can still compete well, in any field. But I do think the stories are written not so much for encouragement, but because the writers are smart enough to know what sells. They see that as our generation ages it wants a model of perennial health and youthful appearances, one that allows it to escape from the reality that aging is just plain tough at times, and then we die.

I am far from a pessimist, but I believe we will never be able to appreciate the advantages of aging, or be receptive of heart to what we *can* learn from this period in our lives, if we enter it with our minds full of fables as to what it is like. Within a year we will be angry, depressed, and convinced we were sold a bill of goods as to how "great" retirement was supposed to be. I have actually known seniors who wore a perpetual smile, and who reported every day how "great it was" to be retired, and who "always" took fabulous trips. Sorry, I have found these folks unbelievable, and a little hard to relate to. But maybe it's just me. They and

I think differently about life, aging and death. I don't believe retirement is 20 to 30 years of highlight films, and people who describe it that way do no one a favor. It seems to me that a senior who seems never to be conscious of the darker side of getting old is very difficult to relate to. I don't want to live in an empty oil drum of pessimism, but I do think we require considerable honesty from one another about the darker side of our aging in order for other persons to empathize with us. Without a balanced perception and communication about our own aging, we may find ourselves always cheering up our ill or discouraged friends, but never truly empathizing with them. There is a danger that we will manage to be cheerful and dreadfully boring at the same time.

On the other hand, I can understand how depression does not sell. Gradual diminishment and unexpected departures are not prime topics expected to excite the enthusiasm of advertisers for *BMW's* or *People* magazine. Even editors of *AARP* magazines must be careful there is not too much black around the edges of their articles. Getting old is not a picnic. It *can* be depressing, so why should we read about it?

O.K. I think I'm done barking. Let's agree, we can share our gripes about how much unrealistic writing there is out there about aging, and we know from experience there is a downside to retirement; but, let's move on to some real, actual, *advantages* to aging.

I wonder if my younger readers have stopped to think about how their elders, or "much elders," have often been able to turn some of the most obvious disadvantages of aging into something constructive? Think with me of the range of age-related difficulties seniors have come to find interesting to talk about with one another: our assorted injuries and ailments, what remedies have worked and what ones haven't, who the better doctors are within a radius of 120 miles, what it is like to go to Urgent Care, or Emergency, what hospitals are best for treating this or that condition, who can best deal with pain, names of physical therapists, acupuncturists, chiropractors, who gives a great massage, who is best for relaxation, who is best for treatment of pain, etc. Senior lists are much longer than this!

Young people may get disgusted with our "health and illness" talk, as if that's all we have to converse about. But they have to remember, health is a *live* topic much of the time for those of us who are aging. Not the *only* thing to talk about, of course, but *live.* And usually interesting to the participants.

Did you know it is fairly common for seniors to kid one another about "having a senior moment?" Yes, well, you may be tired of hearing the phrase if you are younger, but seniors never seem to tire of those words. I love them because it reassures me I am among those who share a similar phase of their lives, who experience a similar forgetting. Both the sharing and the humor helps us feel we may be normal, at least in our forgetfulness. We don't have to feel stupid, or strange, or think of the "senior" stage as a curse, when we are appreciated and accepted for who we are, as we are. One of the true advantages of aging is the way we feel our connections with one another, identify with a similarity of experiences, and in general treat aging with respect, acceptance and humor. I don't know of any other developmental period more defined by heart-felt compassion. Which is as it should be, by the way, if life is to be understood as a journey for developing universal consciousness.

I know there are obvious advantages of aging: Medicare, Social Security, discounted hotels, car rentals, air- fares, and theatre tickets. Older people do get a break for aging. I am interested in talking with you about some of the more subtle advantages of aging, some that come to us as a surprise.

When I first retired, in Portland, Oregon, my wife continued to practice as a clinical psychologist, and I did most of the cooking. An advantage, for me, that many men, or even women, might not think of as advantage, was learning more about grocery shopping and cooking. How to use a variety of herbs, enjoying flavors and smells, cutting out recipes. Knowing where the best sales were, who had the best produce, the best wine selections and discounts. It was in the process of enjoying the advantage of learning about food one day, when an entirely different kind of advantage surprised me.

I was grocery shopping in a specialty store, Trader Joe's. Following its Southern Californian beginnings it planted itself in Northern California, then in the Northwest. It had been discovered by all the "hip" and "cool" generation that loved the good life and unusual and tasty food at good prices. Retirees were not that far behind, with their keen scent for bargains and gourmet foods.

Browsing through the jelly and jam section, I checked out options for marmalade, my usual treatment for morning toast. As I lifted one brand from the shelf and put in into my cart, I noticed an elderly gentleman close to my own age watching my choice. Our eyes met. He appeared to be making up his mind whether to speak to me or not, and for a moment I wondered if I should know him from somewhere. He looked back up the aisle, over his shoulder, and then turned to me again and said, in a deep voice as he pointed to a second brand of marmalade,

"This is a great marmalade, the best I ever had on an English muffin," and he looked at me again, nervously.

I was immensely pleased a fellow shopper, a man, had said something to me. The exchange seemed, well, almost conspiratorial, as if we were agents or something, passing secret information.

"Thanks for mentioning it," I said, meeting his eye and smiling. "I'll have to try it next time I come in."

The man's nervousness began to fall away.

"I hope you don't mind I said something," he said to me.

"Not at all," I responded reassuringly. "I try to pass on good things myself."

He looked relieved and pleased. I thanked him again, and we went our separate ways to do the rest of our shopping.

For my part, I found this exchange strangely and wonderfully engaging. Hey, here was this guy, telling another old guy, about good stuff to put on toast! It doesn't get much better than that. But, then, maybe you think the entire idea of elder bonding through grocery shopping is about as weird as bonding through exchanging recipes, or Chinese pill recommendations for the stomach. What I will say is, perhaps you must become a member of the *Secret Society of the Aging*, especially older men now doing shopping and cooking. Then it may be possible to understand some of our smaller, but wonderfully gratifying, experiences, and why we consider them, advantages of aging.

I wonder at times if the perception we have of getting older depends on the mind set we carry toward it, and into those years. I once stood in a theatre ticket line behind a man I knew slightly from his job as a pharmacist. He was, I would guess, slightly older than I, which meant we both qualified for senior discounts. I loved this neighborhood theatre for its selection of films, its popcorn, its friendliness, and senior rates that started at 60. The less money for tickets, the more for popcorn!

I noted the pharmacist did not request a senior rate for himself or the lady with him and he was charged full adult fare. I thought he might have forgotten to ask, so as I stepped forward in line I caught his eye and laughingly said,

"Aren't you going to take advantage of the senior rate?"

He glared at me and guided his lady friend to an entry aisle, while I was left to wonder what that was all about. I decided, perhaps wrongly, that he did not want attention called to his age. Aging might not have been an advantage in his mind, but demeaning. In any event, he barely spoke to me next time I filled a prescription.

Our capacity to think of our older decades constructively may relate directly to how we have learned to *position* our minds in the years leading up to retirement. If we have disliked our jobs, generally not entered into life fully, curiously, or openly, and we expect retirement to be an idyllic fulfillment of dreams, we are likely to be disillusioned in a very short time.

Similarly, if we have shriveled our capacity for complexity and flexibility of thought and inquiry in the years leading up to retirement, we will employ that same consciousness in how we view the terrain of aging, and see little but bleakness and dry lakes. For such a consciousness Social Security, Medicare, and AARP discounts are statements about decline, not a few of the more tangible advantages of aging.

The small delights I call attention to in this chapter will call to mind many others by older readers who have learned to receive and celebrate life in its many forms, and who have been open to learning from each one. Unfortunately, for those who have been captivated by the illusion of always being able to control life by determination, disdaining aging, or denying its possible teaching, aging becomes a stagnant pool, cluttered by blame and bitterness.

Another of these small, but delightful, conspiratorial adventures occurred recently in Tucson, where my wife and I retired. This time the covert exchange was between a woman and myself.

I had gone to a store specializing in cooking utensils, anything to do with the kitchen. Long dissatisfied with trying to cut thin slices of cheese with a paring knife, I was on a hunt for something better, and not too expensive. After looking through an astonishing array of kitchen utensils, including several that laid claim to being cheese slicers, I finally gave up and asked for assistance. Two employees did their best to show me options, but they knew less about their inventory than I did, so I thanked them and began to poke around other sections of the store.

I was lifting out various items from a gift-pack column when I found a combination marble cutting slab and cheese slicer, with a lever and wire connected. Apparently one took hold of a handle and pulled a thin wire down to slice cheese evenly. I turned the wrapped package over several times, wishing I could see inside, and wondered if I was willing to part with the money required for its purchase. Just then a woman approached me, and from just a few feet away looked into my eyes, though she was obviously very shy. She was very well dressed, attractive, probably in her 70's. She had brown eyes, and a slight tic at the edge of her left eye.

"I've never done this before," she said furtively, "but I saw you looking at the cheese slicing set."

I nodded and replied, "Yes, I've been looking all over for a good thing to use to slice cheese."

"Well, I have one just like this, and it's wonderful. I've had it for 30 years. I bought it in Virginia."

"That's terrific," I responded somewhat dumbly.

"The only trouble I ever had was the wire, so I bought a wire replacement. Then I found out the reason the first wire sagged was because I didn't tighten the little knob. Since then it's worked perfectly."

"Wow!" I said, eloquently.

"As I say, I've never done anything like this before," she repeated, apologetically.

"No, no, I'm really glad you said something," I said reassuringly, finding at last *my* more emotional and authentic voice. "I've been trying to find a cheese slicer that would really work for days." Which was, of course, an exaggeration, but one in the interest of genuine gratitude for this woman and her courage in assisting me.

"Good," she replied with relief. "I know you'll be happy with it."

"Well, thanks again for all your help," I said, and we mutually nodded as we parted.

I realized shortly afterward that our clandestine meeting had not been so secret after all. As I made my way to the purchase counter, I overheard the manager say to her assistant,

"Now the *customers* are doing the selling."

I think you can see the connection older folk often feel with one another, reaching out, finding ways to express our feeling of age-solidarity. I've found these experiences surprising and heart-warming.

I will leave it to other writers to speak of the more structured and obvious advantages to aging. I wish them well, so long as they try mostly to tell the truth. Believe me, if your heart is open, you don't need to gloss over what it means to age. You will welcome it just as it is, the good and the not so good, sometimes even the just plain lousy. There is a lot to learn, and a lot for the heart to grow by, if we just don't blow it. Consciousness never stops expanding unless we attempt to crush change itself, and then we will only dislocate our own bones trying to deny reality.

CHAPTER 13

Consciousness of Mortality

$\mathcal{I}$t is difficult to say how the nature of one's consciousness may be affected by the unavoidable awareness of our mortality. I suppose it depends on how reflective one is. For the reflective, young or old, a consciousness of death may lead to an examination of life priorities. One is likely to feel a closer connection with those they love, as well as hold greater affection for all mortal beings. For those unreflective, I suspect they will intensify their denials and security operations to keep pace with their anxiety.

It's not unusual for some cultures to view the last 20 years of a life as a time for reflective pleasure and peaceful preparation for dying. Consciousness of dying is viewed as part of the life process, resulting in greater appreciation for family and friendships. In the West, where there is far more denial of the reality of death, our culture appears to be more preoccupied with the symbols of youth. As I have pointed out, people are often offended by their own aging, and will not hear of it unless it is disguised as something it could not possibly be in reality.

Occasionally I will meet someone who shares my more Eastern view of aging, that it is a surprisingly satisfying period of change, and, for many of us, of spiritual preparation. What strikes me about these folks is the liveliness of their consciousness. Their engagement with the great questions of existence seem, if anything, to fuel their delight in life, to heighten their curiosity and creativity, and often to enlarge their affections.

As I edge closer to my death, I am appreciating the seamless character of what I think of as my spiritual journey. Nothing seems separately "religious" to me any longer. I am likely to bring as much delight to any variety of experiences I might have in the next 24 hours as I would to a designated religious setting. It makes less and less sense to divide life into sacred and profane, or religious and secular. After all, we are bringing our bodies and spirit to each event of life. If we are engaged with our hearts, we *are* our religion *in* those, and *through* those, events; we don't *have* a religion. Even if we are somewhat conscious of being carriers of the Spirit, it is not incumbent on us to do "God talk." In fact "God talk" may run counter to what we have come to believe about who God is and who we are. Ultimately, we are simply bearers of giftedness and gratitude who take delight in all of life. If there is any light in us, we will be less conscious of it than others will be, so what is there to talk about? We live without the requirement, wish, or need to wear religious name tags.

Retirement may be what many in the East think it is, a remarkable time for attending to health, family, and an increasing sense of oneness with All that Is. I certainly value the earlier, more intense years of my life. They had their own function and purpose. But I don't feel I have lost anything by leaving them behind. While aging years do have to contend with sometimes debilitating illnesses, I have come to learn they are absolutely full of opportunities for enlarging our hearts and expanding our consciousness. It is because it is a time for preparation for death, that our hearts become all the more grateful for each day we have, each relationship. And for many of us, our greatest joy is the gift of an ever-enlarging, intimate sense of Presence.

I want to share three experiences rooted in mortality that have affected the course of my life and shaped the nature of my faith. Perhaps at the end of the chapter you may want to record *your* experiences with mortality and how those experiences may have changed your faith and thinking.

Two surgical events in adult life made me a more conscious being. I felt I was wiser after each of them. Wiser because the results were unexpected. Here is a meditation I recorded in my journal as I approached surgery for removal of a pacemaker and a lead that had failed:

There is a voice in me that does not think about God at all, and which, in the face of surgery, and the fear of dying, considers faith and the hereafter irrelevant. Irrelevant to the immediate task: getting ready for surgery, and then getting through it.

This is the voice that has to do with putting my affairs in order, the voice of pragmatic love for my wife and my children, not wanting them to be left with a mess, a chaos of papered disorder, a labyrinth of uncertainty. My practical, fearful, egocentric, controlling, agnostic defiant self is running this show. And I believe it *should* at the moment.

Then there is another voice, which is also me. It is like some great whale, making its 5000 miles journey to give birth, surfacing now and then for air, perhaps visible only by sea water spurts, blowing high in the sky. It is the voice of depth, of spiritual destiny, of mystery. This voice is ready to sound, ready to leap from the sea, tail flashing. Why call this God, and diminish it? Call it everything there is, everything there ever was, or will be, the whale, closest thing to love we know.

That was my first less serious surgical brush with mortality. It intensified my affections for my wife and children. I wrote poems about that heart deepening, a not unusual expansion of consciousness for those who are forced by failures in their systems to realize what's really important and dear in life. But the surgical event also taught me more about the respective validity of different voices we carry in our consciousness. The practical voice. The voice that wants to make sure others we love are taken care of if we should die. The mystical voice that for me was surprisingly confident, knowing, and even ecstatic. I learned to give some space to each of them, and not behave as if I should expect only *one* voice, or listen to only one voice, when keenly aware of the possibility of my death.

I had asked the surgeon to get the pacemaker leads out of my body. I didn't want the hardware in there. But I failed to grasp the nature of leads. Once they are placed in the heart through a vein, they are built to stay there safely, to use their prongs to resist movement. That was why I could play aggressive basketball and tennis and feel the leads would not cause a rupture. I was given local anesthesia, so I was relatively conscious and became aware the surgeon was having difficulty pulling out the first lead. Despite being heavily sedated, the procedure was still very painful. The surgeon succeeded in extracting one lead, but he told me he wouldn't attempt to take out the other one. It was just too difficult for him and too painful for me. During this procedure I listened to the voice of confidence in my excellent surgeon and his two assistants, who kept up a steady banter with me during the surgery. I listened to the voice of gratitude that I was in such good hands at such a significant time in my aging. It is at the edge of our mortality when we are likely to hear voices we may never have heard.

My second brush with mortality was a more serious one, when it was thought I had lymphoma. I referred to aftermath of the surgery in a previous chapter, "Spiritual Agnosticism." Fortunately, the final diagnosis, made after almost three hours of surgery, was, no cancer. I had lymphangioma, a non-cancerous bunching of renegade lymph sacs, disconnected from the rest of the lymph system. Still, the surgery required a bowel resection and bypass, and the removal of two feet of my large intestine and a small section of my colon. I was hospitalized a week and the recovery period after that was one year.

I discovered through that experience how dependent my mystical orientation was on the existing energy available in my body, specifically as it relates to the heart and intuition. It was not that I *had* no beliefs for the long months following surgery. They were still tucked away in my mind and deeper being I am sure. But I could not *access* them in a way familiar to me. I had no energy to *experience* what I felt to be the Presence of God. In that sense I was "dead to God." While a great contribution to my understanding of the complex nature of personal faith, and how it functions in some of us who are grounded in our bodies, the discovery of its absence, and my dependency on my body for a vital faith, was accompanied by depression and great feelings of abandonment.

Because this crisis of faith, brought on by the threat of death and the failure of my energy system, is addressed elsewhere in this book, I will only say the experience was a hard way to learn more about faith and the threat of mortality. Out of that zombie-like darkness that I sometimes thought would never end, I was cared for and prayed for by those who loved me, family and friends. Eventually a confidence emerged in my consciousness that God was there, even when I had lived in darkness. I came to understand it is impossible to get rid of light, even in the worst of the darkness.

Following is a meditation I wrote when I gave credence to the serious possibility of my death. Keep in mind its metaphorical meaning, rather than its literal meaning:

When I am gone I want my family to wear black.

I want them to see the tiny beads of light emerging from their dark jackets, their blouses, skirts, their hats, their black shoes. Light, lifting off everything black, as if emerging from tiny little caves, revolving molecules in a glistening dance. I want my family to be in awe of how much light there is, how much has been hiding all along, only to be revealed as body life ends.

I want my family to notice how discomforted they become as they realize how close their tears of grief are to a remembrance that makes them smile, to laughter hiding away in their throats and upper chests. I want them to notice their hearts, how connected their hearts and minds are, quieted in saying goodbye, so connected to the peacefulness of a gathering blue pool, how vivid, and even playful, memories become. Each memory, as it appears, is a ripple in a slight tide that began somewhere else, someplace deep, forming itself in eternity before it ever reached our shores of recollection, like a song about its particular bonding with eternity.

I want my family to wear black because it is such a lie. It makes a statement about blandness, how alike we all are, when the truth of things is how beads of light are always escaping the prisons of darkness, assuming an infinite variety of colors, turning like a child's bubbles. The truth is not uniformity, but the diversity of our lives and faith, our memories, our way of uniquely recalling what belongs to us, and in some ways, no one else. It is our particular history and it is our shared history together, but seen through our different eyes.

I like black because it is background for stars and moonlight, it is for fireworks in the sky, the best always saved for last, the triumphant notes not yet heard. They belong together, darkness and light, sorrow and celebration, if all life is one and continuous. The life I am in now is inseparable from the life in you, save for the momentary differences of clay, habitation and expression.

It is hard to stifle joy. How will anyone else know, that while you truly do mourn, your grief initiates a deep rumbling of soul that creates rippling in your earth body, and the surfacing of unexpected delight and joy? It is almost an embarrassment to our minds how intimately all of life is connected, and yet the mind has not noticed this intimacy, something the soul has known from the beginning of time.

Let death not serve as the signal for a frantic scavenger hunt for every conceivable good attribute that might define one who has died. Let death make space for some quiet time where there *are* no words, when we will be able to let our hearts and minds roam, to find the balance of joy and grief, to find the realistic appreciation for the one now gone on ahead. To find easily gratitude for how we have been influenced by this one life.

When I am gone, wear black, because all of you who know me will think, "This is what he would have wanted, a last chance to celebrate a final paradox: how out of darkness comes light."

One more story, not of my mortality edge, but that of a friend's edge. I was deeply honored to have been asked by my tennis competitor friend to spend time with him. At first just talking, visiting a beautiful Catholic Mission Church, at his request teaching him meditation. Then, sitting with him, his wife, and often his married daughter, during his last few weeks of life in hospice. I visited every other day until the last two or three weeks. We meditated quietly. Sometimes I brought a brief reading from the Psalms, because he and his family were Roman Catholic in their faith. Other times we might talk or be silent. When the family asked if I would be willing to attend daily the last three weeks, I said I would. Bill and I were connected in powerful ways I accepted, even if I could not explain why. We were friends and I loved him from my heart. I came to feel deeply connected with his wife and daughter. My soul was being affected and changed by my experience with Bill and his family in his body's dying.

Our meditative time of silent breathing and heart consciousness worked well for Bill and his family. The silent concentration created a respectful bond of respect among us. It became a channel for our hearts to open further, the heart of my friend, that of his wife and married daughter, and my own. The meditation bond with Spirit released a quiet but powerful energy, making possible our consciousness of many other beautiful events during the few weeks my friend would have left.

The longer these visitations went on, and the deeper our experiences became, the less I knew what to expect of meditation, of myself, or the physical condition of my friend. I felt at times like I was trying vainly to put myself back into two very old roles I had given up many years before, like attempting to cram myself into my World War II paratrooper uniform. It was not going to work. Whatever would happen in hospice, whatever I might read, in addition to silent meditation, whatever audible prayer I might offer for the sake of the family, had to be right. It had to emerge from my consciousness in some natural, organic way. It had to fit the dynamic we were *all* experiencing, and not be an imposed, artificial form I might fall back on just because it was familiar.

I asked for the prayers of my wife and two tennis buddies I trusted who loved Bill, and their wives. I asked them to pray I would be strengthened to deal with my own grief, since I was quite shaky, and to say and do the "right thing." The morning after I first asked them for their prayers, I found myself choosing a reading from the New Testament for the first time. It was the Apostle Paul's famous treatise on the nature of love. As I read the selection, a portion of the thirteen chapter of First Corinthians, I noticed Bill's daughter Kathy was silently weeping. She and her mother looked at one another knowingly. Kathy told me later the passage I had selected was the one her father had read to her at her wedding, when he gave her to her future husband. I don't think I chose that passage by accident. I called and thanked my buddies for their prayers.

For the Corinthian reading, Bill may not have been conscious. His eyes were closed during the entire meditation. But his Spirit knew!

I was startled by a dream one night during my earliest visitations to the hospice. The face that appeared was clearly that of Bill's. In the dream he had arranged a huge banquet, and he had prepared all the food. He was taking great delight in seeing people eat and enjoy themselves. I believed I had been given a message about my friend's deepest essence. In the life of the Spirit, he was the great giver of feasts. The host. Significantly, during our earliest conversations Bill told me that in his working life one of his jobs overseas was to be the host for dinners honoring his sale's staff, or introducing customers to new products. I came to believe that at a level of the Spirit, even as his body lost its life, Bill's Spirit was hosting a banquet to which we had been invited. We would receive

a spiritual nurturance that we could not yet imagine. I found a way to
kid him about this more profound aspect of his nature. At first he joked
about it, put the image away with a wave of his hand. But eventually he
came to terms with the reality of his deepest nature. He was sponsor of
a banquet, giver of gifts and blessings. I certainly experienced my time
with Bill that way, and with his family. I hope you, the reader, will feel
upon reading these words about my friend, that you have been invited
to his banquet.

Toward the last, one day as I came in, and we were preparing to
meditate, Bill looked right at me and said,

"The banquet goes on, doesn't it?"

"Yes, Bill," I said, "the banquet goes on."

The day before Bill died, I was sitting on the bed next to him, my
thigh against his on one side, and my hand holding against his other
thigh firmly on the other side. His eyes were closed the entire time, and
he was very quiet. Donna said he had had a difficult night. The two of us
sat with Bill in this silent energy. The form of our meditation, entirely
silent,once again, found its own way to be. Sometimes my eyes were
closed, at other times they were looking at Bill. Looking, yet not looking,
a strange kind of unfocused resting of my eyes upon his being.

The first vision which came to me as I looked was of my friend's
earthly awareness and consciousness. It was connected with the life he
had lived. I saw him totally at peace in his body consciousness. No rest-
lessness. He had come to know there was no more for him to do in this
earthly life. He had completed his course, fulfilled his intention on this
earth. Any anxieties about incompletion because of the relatively young
age at which he was dying, were gone.

The second vision I had was of Bill's Spirit. I could see it wished to
escape the earthly body, which now had become less a home and more a

confinement. Some of the Essence energy already had, it seemed to me, escaped and drifted into the room, all about the area over his bed. The power of that energy seemed to me palpable, and I could feel enormous warmth in my hands and body. The departing Spirit had a gray, or light brown, color to it. I talked with a Buddhist teacher I trust about this vision and she said, "Yes, like dust." Light, filmy dust, not ordinarily visible to the naked eye.

I understand the Spirit has had a 64-year association with this particular body. There are certain attachments and connections that require relinquishing, releases by both the dying body and the Spirit, before the Spirit can re-unite with the Oneness of all Being. The Spirit has both gratitude and grief for the loving association with this unusual body it has inhabited for so many years. Death and parting take time. A kind of painful patience is required for the process to unfold. Nevertheless, the parting was relatively rapid, inasmuch as Bill officially died the next day, a day I did not visit.

My third experience in that sacred setting, the day before Bill officially died, was auditory: I heard choral singing in the background. At first it was a small chorus, then swelling to a much larger and beautiful one. I thought of the choral singing as welcoming my friend, Bill, into the Kingdom of Heaven. I raised the question with myself, might I have been hearing an angelic chorus? I shared my vision with Donna before I left that day.

Did I create these visions of what might happen as we die, or at least as Bill died? I hope so. I hope a Divine Consciousness existed within me at that moment in time in the hospice, a consciousness that permitted me to be graced with visions of spiritual reality right in front of my eyes. A consciousness that may have graced my soul with insight into the ultimate nature of death and reunion Being, and etch the experience into my consciousness as a template for my own faith.

Bill and his family gave me many gifts in my time with them at the hospice, but no gift was more remarkable than the last vision that re-markable day: a vision of what our transition may be like as we move from earth form to the liberation of Spirit. Death is a *real* word, but it is not the *last* word, for my final vision that remarkable day was a simple image: The full light cannot be released until the vessel that holds it is broken.

Faith is a capacity

to imagine a re-assembly of ruins into spacious and fresh forms

CHAPTER 14

Remembering Kindness

You are never too young to remember kindnesses toward you, nor are you ever too old. Perhaps we have greater opportunity when we are older to reach back into our memory for kind deeds or gestures toward us. We have a longer history to draw upon, and if we are retired we also have the leisure time for reflections. I think, too, that it must be a natural part of an older developmental stage that we may have touching memories from our younger days that surface unexpectedly. But if we are young, it will be a lifelong gift to ourselves if we consciously develop the habit of cultivating a receptive mind, recalling kind words or deeds toward us during our pre-adolescent and adolescent periods of our lives. Unfortunately, it is possible to close the door to touching and pleasant memories, especially if we have created a consciousness that cultivates memories of real or exaggerated victimization or absences of kindnesses we expected. Depending on our mind set, we may censor touching memories of kindness, or simply exclude them from our rigid system of thinking; or, we may teach ourselves to be open to these healthy and wonderful memories, even if much of our life has been difficult or even traumatic.

The recollection of kindnesses is healing, whether we are young or old, or somewhere in between. We need our hearts to be touched, and we need our private smiles and our tears of gratitude, if our consciousness is to evolve and our spiritual faith is to be as lively and compassionate as our memories of kindness. That phenomenon, of the part our heart plays in the creation of an imaginative, generous faith, is why I have included a chapter in this book that focuses on kindness toward us as a spiritual gift.

I spent the first six years of my life in a little spot called Hodge, next to highway 66 on the Mojave Desert in California. Hodge no longer exists. With an extensive train station terminal only 10 miles East, in Barstow, and a three-shift station 15 miles to the West in Victorville, Hodge would eventually become redundant to Santa Fe operations. The only remnant that remained of the town when I went back some 30 years ago was a brick building. It had once been a one-room school house for eight grades. Now it was a run-down residence for one or more families. The Santa Fe train station was gone. The house built along the track for agent-telegraphers and their families was no longer there, nor was a house on an adjoining lot where the Hispanic section gang foreman and his family lived. What was not gone was an important memory of Hodge and a boy who lived next door to us, Enrique. Enrique may not have been his name, but I will call him that to tell you a story of kindness.

The principal of the elementary school in Hodge was a young woman from the city who came out for the school year to teach its 30 or so students. She lived in a frame house next to the school. On a late August day Mother and I visited her to see if I could be enrolled in first grade, since I was six months younger than the ordinary admitting age of six. My fear of being in a new environment was offset somewhat by liking the principal. Mother was successful in persuading the principal I was ready for elementary school. That turned out not to be the case, but my acceptance into the class pleased my mother. When classes began I made my way up the path, which was across Highway 66 from our house. There were three other children in first grade.

Enrique, one of the section gang foreman's children who lived next door to us, waited with me the first morning we left for school. He was probably 10 or 11. Each of our mothers stood by our sides to see us off, making sure no traffic was coming on Route 66 before sending us across. Highway 66 was the main highway going east from Los Angeles, but not nearly so busy as it became over time, requiring the building of a separate freeway that bypassed where Hodge had once existed. Enrique was rather quiet until I got to know him while we walked to school together and back. After a time it was not unusual for us to tease one another, or for him to give me a head start, and then both of us racing to see who could get to the edge of the highway first. He took very seriously his self-adopted role of watching out for me, and after a week or so, our mothers no longer felt the need to wait for us and escort us across the highway. Enrique took on that responsibility.

We had a cow that my father milked, and he thought a fruit jar of milk, with yummy cream on top, was what I needed to drink every day to be healthy. Each day I would take a sandwich, an apple or orange, and my jar of milk to school in a bag. Returning home, having disposed of the paper bag from morning, I carried only the empty milk jar in my hands. One day, as Enrique and I were returning home through the grease-woods and sage, one of us challenged the other, "Race you!" I was off and running as Enrique let me get my usual lead. I tore down the path, as fast as a five year old can dash, when suddenly I tripped and sprawled into the sand just off the path. I must have hit a rock with my milk jar and it broke. A piece of it slashed my forehead just above one eye.

Enrique had seen me fall. He rushed to where I was holding my hand to my forehead. When he saw the broken glass and blood seeping through my fingers, he realized what had happened. Without hesitation he pulled off his white T-shirt and said,

"Here, let me put this on your forehead."

I don't think he attempted to tie it at the back, but he held the T-shirt against my brow with one hand, and lifted me to my feet with the other. Enrique began to walk me down the path, his left arm around my back to steady me, his right hand pressing the makeshift bandage against my brow. Slowly we walked to where the path ended. After he looked closely both ways, he guided me across the highway, and we made our way to my family's kitchen door.

Mother, already at the window, and expecting us from school, saw us stumbling up the path to our house and knew something was wrong, Enrique with no shirt, and holding a white garment against my head. She went to the screen door, and shrieked as she saw blood on my face. She threw open the screen door and dashed down the steps, kneeling to hold me and look at my wound. Enrique told her what had happened as she lifted the T-shirt away and looked at my injury. She could tell that while it was bleeding quite a lot, the slash did not look critical. I might not require a trip into Barstow for stitches. Mother thanked Enrique, and a next day delivered a cleaned, pressed, and very white T-Shirt next door to his mother.

What I remember after all these years was the look of distress and concern on Enrique's face when he saw I had hurt myself. What

I remember was how immediately he pulled off his T-shirt and held it against my injury. I remember our slow journey the short distance to the highway, his arm around me, with his other hand holding the makeshift bandage to my forehead.

I left Hodge the following year when my father took a station shift in Victorville, so I have no idea what happened to Enrique. He has become one of these anonymous persons, whose names I no longer remember, who have left the imprint of their kindness on me forever.

There are not a large number of memories I recall from my early childhood. Why should this one have stood out? I believe it is because my heart was undeniably and permanently affected in those few dramatic moments when I was five years old, by Enrique's concern and kindness. When I first wrote of my memory of this incident, I was amazed to find tears coming to my eyes. I had a picture of Enrique's concerned expression in my mind, and more tears rolled down my cheeks. Now, as I write again, more than 70 years after the incident, I feel the same stirring in my heart, a filling, and tears of gratitude once more.

I don't think my remembrance of the many kindnesses in my life is particularly exceptional. I would not be at all surprised if my readers, at this moment, are discovering emotions stirring, your hearts bringing to mind acts of kindness on your behalf over a lifetime.

Many of the kindnesses we remember seem to have been offered by persons outside our family, often by strangers. Why should we remember them? I wonder if it is because we have many complicated feelings about our families and how they have affected our consciousness. With strangers, the kindness they offered may have been unrelated to any possible expectation of return. The kindness came to us unexpectedly, and with no strings attached. We had no history with the stranger to have built up expectations, and therefore no history of the inevitability of

some disappointment. The energies of a stranger's kindness are uncluttered by our mind set, and the memories of it can go straight to our
hearts without interference, if we will permit their journey.

That was certainly the case for another of my experiences with a
stranger that has permanently affected both my heart and my thinking.
It happened during World War II. I had completed paratrooper jump
training and was stationed in Fort Bragg, North Carolina. Each graduate was given a short leave, and I arranged to take a train to Chicago,
then Minneapolis, to see a cousin who was in nursing school. I arrived
in Minneapolis on a very cold, snowy day in December, the day before
Christmas. It was already late, 6:00, and I still needed to make my way
to the "Y," where some 200 servicemen and women would be sleeping
that night.

I was standing on a street corner under a light, wondering where I
would get a bite to eat before striking out for the "Y." A man in his 50's
stood next to me, waiting for the light to change, wearing a heavy top-
coat and a felt hat. He must have noticed how miserably cold I appeared
to be, and that I was a serviceman. I think I must have been emotionally
miserable, too. It was Christmas Eve, and I was by myself in a city I had
never seen before. Next day my cousin and I would meet and go by train
into Chicago to spend Christmas with her family and other of our rela-
tives. But tonight I was alone, 1500 miles from my divorced parents, and
18 years old. The man next to me may have surmised I was alone on this
Christmas eve when he spoke to me almost shyly,

"You know, my wife and I are Jewish, but we would welcome you
to our house for dinner and a place to stay, if you don't have any plans
tonight."

There was a lot I didn't know when I was 18, including anything
about either the Jewish faith or the Christian faith, since I was raised in

a home that ignored religion. But there was one thing I did know at 18. I knew when someone was being kind to me. I said "no," politely to the gracious man, who had just finished working and was on his way home. I told him about my appointment to meet my cousin in the morning, and my plan to sleep at the YMCA. After we crossed the street, he went off in one direction, and I in another toward the YMCA. As I walked along in the snow and cold, inside I was warmer than I had been since arriving in Minneapolis on a cold and snowy Christmas Eve. That man and I had what was probably a one minute conversation, and its memory has stayed in my consciousness ever since. There are kindnesses we never forget. They bridge differences of religious practice and belief. They bridge differences of race, gender, sexual orientation and nationality.

Why have I written of kindness rather than love? I think because the word "love" is very much like the word, "God." Both are used indiscriminately, often casually, and on occasion with only a crass commercial or political intention. Which is not to say we must give the terms up, but that we may have to start somewhere else in order to come back to them in a way that truly honors their essential depth. I think of myself as beginning with "kindness" this way, coming in the back door of the house, through the screen door of the porch that fronted houses I grew up in on the desert. But I do know a function of the screen door of kindness memories, is to get us into the house of gratitude. For it is gratitude that often softens and opens our hearts so we begin to see more often through the eyes of compassion and understanding, and less through the eyes of suspicion and judgment. What I believe is that there cannot *be* a telling spiritual journey without a continuing presence of gratitude.

As disagreeable as some events might be, when our hearts open up to embracing life, many of us find ourselves grateful for what we have learned through the worst of them. At the time, as I say, the experience may be angering, full of grief, and otherwise most painful, whether it is physical distress, the breakup of our families, or the loss of loved ones. But over time, unless we cling to our beliefs in how life "should be," and maintain a stance of bitterness, it is possible for us to learn through experiencing events we cannot control, and the dissolution of a faith that probably needed some reconstruction for us to become kinder beings.

To return to our memories of kindness: Notice how you will have a memory of kindness, followed by a charge, or warmth, in your heart, then how this charge spreads to your brain, and then throughout your body. That is why some say a memory of goodness originates in our open hearts, and then creates a mental memory that is capable of charging up the entire human cellular system. Reflect on this during your own meditation, and you will see why, in speaking of love, I have begun by talking of tangible acts of human kindness that *affect* our hearts, that take us into the house of gratitude and compassion.

In one of the more remarkable ecstatic experiences of my later years, a powerful memory flooded my mind very early in the morning while I was still in bed. I had been in Guatemala 20 years earlier for language study. I had been browsing through a native arts and crafts market, when I saw a woman sitting on the ground in her stall, which was customary, most not having tables to show their wares. Off to the side sat two of her children, a girl about 8 and a boy, perhaps 10. Both were sitting there stolidly, scarcely looking at the crowd passing by. The woman held a blue and red scarf with one hand at her neck, the scarf thrown round her shoulders. With her other hand she held her husband's outstretched hand. He lay on the ground, an empty liquor bottle at his side, moaning and making unintelligible, almost ritualistic sounds. His wife looked into the faces of those passing by, in the event anyone should take an interest in buying a shawl she had woven, or colorful placemats and napkins.

I recalled how customary it was to use alcohol in ancient Mayan and Inca religious ceremonies, some conducted thousands of feet into the mountains to appease and appeal to mountain deities. Indian priests also used tobacco, smoking, sprinkling ash and fresh tobacco intentionally on objects brought to them for sacrifice, and onto the fire. As for the alcohol, they would take a drink, sprinkle some of the liquid on the sacrificial objects, and then onto the ground, take another drink and spit it onto the sacred ground.

What came to me in my vision, or my imagination—it does not really matter which—was that this drunken man in the stall, this husband and father, was still hanging onto an aspect of a ceremony that had once been very meaningful and powerful, alcohol. It was all he had left to claim from the role and dignity of a priestly or shamanic heritage, all that was left of the form of his particular religious practice.

When I had this vision of what he had lost, and the harmful way the use of alcohol had been distorted, I felt enormous sorrow. I think I tapped into my sorrow, and the sorrow so many experience, when the form of faith that had nourished and given them identity and meaning had to die. I was terribly surprised by my grief and puzzled. I asked of God, or perhaps no one,

"What am I supposed to get from this vision?"

I asked the same question several times, not really expecting an answer. Then I saw how the Guatemalan Indian woman kept one of her hands on her drunken husband's hand, while with her other hand she held her scarf together at her neck. The answer to my question came in a simple, single phrase:

When form comes to an end, love remains.

I got up from my bed and wrote all this vision down. I felt a further opening and softening of my heart, my entire body charging with energy.

When form comes to an end, love remains.
A statement about the ultimate nature of our existence:
All forms dissolve. Only love prevails.

CHAPTER 15

Learning How to Celebrate Most Everything

This morning at breakfast I was reading the newspaper, giving only minimal attention to an article about how a NASA jet plane had made its last flight to a desert retirement field. It had been used to train astronauts for weightlessness in space. Now it would be stripped for its usable parts and its body placed in permanent storage at an Arizona graveyard for military planes. Let me quote from the last two paragraphs of the article:

> The aircraft made its final landing at Ellington Field last Friday afternoon, where it was greeted by two Air Force fire engines. With their lights going, the fire trucks escorted the plane down the runway. They pulled ahead as the aircraft approached Hangar 990, and then opened up their water hoses, spraying an arch of water over the plane as it completed its final voyage.

I was astounded to find that as I read the final paragraphs, tears came to my eyes. Later I would wonder why that might be. Just getting older? Less defended and more sentimental? Could be. But as I looked into the experience more deeply, I recognized how celebrations differ.

I was familiar with celebrating victories for myself or my team on the tennis court. The energetic charge for those celebrations was heady, brain located, one might say closely connected to my ego. There were other celebrations where the energetic charge supporting it felt deeper in my body, as in honoring colleagues who had left a heritage of wisdom and scholarship to those of us still teaching or practicing the healing arts. More clearly, there were celebrations of gratitude and affection within the family, as when those present honored my wife at a surprise 60th birthday celebration, and the charge centered powerfully in our hearts when words struggled to be born.

My unexpected emotional response, as I read of the final flight of an old jet plane that had done its duty faithfully in the interests of the larger reach of our human quest, may have touched into *my* aging and flight of my last journey. It might have been a silent recognition of the dignity possible for those who see themselves as part of a higher quest, a usefulness beyond the limited material of their own egos and bodies. But I suspect what most touched me, as I read of the fire truck crew bringing in the Jet KC-135 for its final runway trip, was a visual image of the arch of water the crew sprayed above the plane as it completed its final voyage.

The watered arc of celebration pointed to an enterprise much larger than the firemen who pointed the nozzles. It celebrated the exploration of space on behalf of all human beings. At an unconscious level I think space exploration touches into our longings to comprehend the awesomeness of our beginnings. It embraces our urge to return to the impossible mystery of our oneness with the Creator. Is not this the ultimate celebration, where all earthly beings are united beyond our nationalistic self-interest, beyond the provincialism of our immaturities, when we understand ourselves to be joined in our quest for oneness with Being?

A few memorable pictures are embedded in most minds of celebrations that may only be called grotesque: Adolph Hitler doing a little jig in the presence of his Nazi generals as he congratulates himself in Paris on the fall of France in World War II. Or think of the Bin Laden smile, as he recounts with a few intimates how his plan to kill thousands in the 9/11 twin towers, was even more successful than he had calculated and imagined.

Apparently we were created to celebrate. And if we do not evolve to celebrate Being, if we do not become large enough to celebrate the lives of others, we still must celebrate *something*. We may get stuck in self-celebration, not so much in an honest appreciation for our nature and skills, but with inordinate pre-occupation with our appearances, popularity, and acquisitions. Each celebration of how we look, or what we possess, eventually fades, to be followed by fear and uncertainty.

Self-celebration carries with it a long-term cultural imprisonment in the United States when we become increasingly dependent on our need to look youthful, much to the satisfaction of industries profiting most from our anxieties. Companies and surgeons who cater to our fear of aging take home the money.

When was the last time you heard someone say they found many reasons to *celebrate* getting old? When I first heard a woman my age say she liked her wrinkles the way they were because she felt she had earned them, I was impressed. Here was someone who understood aging as a period of life to be welcomed for its own gifts. Here was someone who defined herself as "attractive" because she genuinely felt that way about her nature and history. How do you sculpt dignity? Does it not have more to do with character and generosity of outlook than with Botox? So it has been historically in the Far East, where the aging and aged are honored for the wisdom they have acquired, not because they look "ten years younger than they are."

Those who center in their hearts will always find reasons to celebrate, to thank God for one aspect of life after another. Those centered in their heads, who have a fixed notion as to what life *should* be, are more likely to experience unrelenting disappointment. Eventually they become cynical, see little or no reason to celebrate at all. It is a desolate landscape that is governed by a perception there is no one to thank, no one outside an angry self, and that there is very little worth celebrating. I believe it is simply a reality that the larger our consciousness becomes, the more reasons we find to celebrate. It does not take much. Nor did it for the Psalmist, who said,

"This is the day that the Lord has made. Let us rejoice and be glad in it."

POSTSCRIPT

After my wife read the chapter, "If You Are God," she said she liked the chapter, but she didn't like the word, "God." Our conversation went something like this:

"I liked your revision, most of it's good," Linda said.

"Wow! I thought I really nailed it this time," I replied.

"No, it flows better. I just didn't like the word, 'God.'"

"Well I do, and I'm going to keep it. So what word would you use?" I asked.

"I like 'Spirit,' she replied.

"I *used* 'Spirit.' *And* 'Being'. And 'the One.' Quite a few different terms. I think you prefer 'Spirit' because it sort of floats around, a wisp."

"Yes," Linda agreed, nodding. " 'Spirit' is fluid instead of fixed."

"A more feminine word," I suggested

"Exactly. When you use the word, 'God' I get a sense of an object, not a subject.

"And I like 'God,' I said, "because it's masculine," aware I had not previously realized *why* I liked the sound and feeling of 'God.' So it was more than simple familiarity from its use in my Christian tradition origins. Perhaps my resonance with the word "God" in referring to The Divine was a typically *male* one.

"Look," I continued. "I feel I've used other terms broadly enough so that the nuances of what we both believe, that The Divine is a living Presence, will spill over into the consciousness of anyone who reads the book. I think they're capable of reconstructing the word, "God," just as we are.

Linda looked reflective, and nodded. "Probably. But I still don't like the term."

I laughed. "And I do. It points up one of the things I'm trying to do with the book, refurbish the term, 'God,' so that people who are asking serious questions about spirituality see they don't have to be stuck with fixed beliefs that *locate* God, that actually imprison the Divine inside the walls of their own unexamined thinking."

One of the things I most value about the character of our highly individualistic faith, Linda's and mine, is its dynamic quality. Our different faith energies and the ideas they form create the possibility for rich interactions from time to time. In this case the interaction was provocative enough that I wanted to include it in this book.

READER COMMENTS ABOUT TEDDY BEARS

"Your description of energetic, embedded oneness with Being that is beyond dogma is articulate and inspirational."

—**Gregory Johanson,**
Ph.D, author, theologian, psychotherapist.

"The most insightful and thought-provoking book I've read in 20 years. It is sure to spark controversy."

—**Clifford A. Winter,**
M.A., theology; retired business owner.

"The concepts of kindness, celebration and the advantages of aging underscore the book's tenderness—an un-dogmatic and refreshing look at what I once rejected 40 years ago as a driven-away Catholic."

—**Cass McGovern,**
Ph.D., Counseling;
retired reference librarian.

"Not for the faint of heart...For Don it is simple: God is Being and consciousness...Don is more qualified than Dawkins or Harris, in my humble opinion, to explore the edges and limits of faith."

—**The Reverend Michael Robinson,**
A review in *The Standard-Times,*
New Bedford, Mass.
September 1, 2007.

"Clarity and depth inspired me on initial reading. Yet beneath the large thoughts lies the working mystery of love—my most favorite subject."

—**Brugh Joy,**
Spiritual teacher and author.

"There is depth to this material that takes time to sift through. A special kind of balance between confidence and humility occurs when realizing, and saying to one's self, 'I AM GOD.' A body awareness of uniqueness yet simultaneously belonging to the mystery of a larger consciousness."

—**Shirley Erickson,**
Spiritual counselor.

"In this age of religious intolerance it is refreshing to hear a voice of reason and compassion."

—**Solala Towler,**
Editor, *The Empty Vessel*,
a Taoist journal.

"An exceptional piece of work addressing the need to cultivate an inner, thoughtful spirituality, as over against dependency on externalized authority and dogma."

—**Steve Shear,**
Patent attorney, artist.

"An excellent guide for seeking the 'God within," and finding one's own individual path to a deeper faith."

—**Arthur Solomon,**
Ph.D, professor.

Printed in the United States
104426LV00004B/1-102/P

9 781587 367847